Berlitz

MALLORCA

POCKET GUIDE

Walking Eye
mobile app

Discover the world's best destinations with the Insight Guides Walking Eye app, available to download for free in the App Store and Google Play.

The container app provides easy access to fantastic free content on events and activities taking place in your current location or chosen destination, with the possibility of booking, as well as the regularly-updated Insight Guides travel blog: Inspire Me. In addition, you can purchase curated, premium destination guides through the app, which feature local highlights, hotel, bar, restaurant and shopping listings, an A to Z of practical information and more. Or purchase and download Insight Guides eBooks straight to your device.

TOP 10 ATTRACTIONS

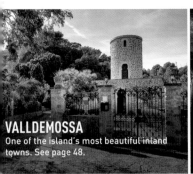

VALLDEMOSSA
One of the island's most beautiful inland towns. See page 48.

COVES DEL DRAC
Beautifully presented caves with one of the world's largest underground lakes. See page 76.

MONESTIR DE LLUC
Wonderful views and soul-lifting singing in Mallorca's most holy site. See page 59.

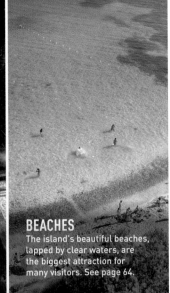

BEACHES
The island's beautiful beaches, lapped by clear waters, are the biggest attraction for many visitors. See page 64.

DEIÀ
Once the home of Robert Graves and still one of the prettiest villages on the island. See page 52.

FUNDACIÓ PILAR I JOAN MIRÓ
Experience the life and work of one of Spain's most famous artists. See page 41.

CAN PRUNERA
Lean about Modernisme in this museum in Sóller. See page 54.

SERRA DE TRAMUNTANA
Beautiful walks in this World Heritage Site. See page 45.

SINEU MARKET
This traditional Wednesday-morning farmers' market is arguably the island's best. See page 70.

PALMA'S CATHEDRAL
Dominating the city and the harbour, this marvellous Gothic cathedral is a stunning sight. See page 29.

A PERFECT DAY

9.00am

Breakfast
In Palma, have breakfast at the trendy and photogenic Mise En Place in Plaça Major, where a delicious array of breakfast options (homemade pastries, cooked breakfasts, fruit pots) awaits you. It's slightly hidden, but well worth the extra time spent searching for it.

10.00am

In search of Chopin
Take the road that runs about 10km (6 miles) through olive and almond groves to Valldemossa and La Real Cartuja, where you can visit the apartments in which George Sand and Frédéric Chopin once stayed. In the adjoining palace, Palau del Rei Sanxo, recitals of Chopin's music are held throughout the day.

12 noon

Sweet treat
Explore the town and stop for coffee and a *coca de patata*, a sweet local pastry, in the Carrer Blanquera.

1.00pm

Delightful Deià
Continue on the scenic coast road to Deià, a honey-coloured little town that was home to poet Robert Graves and still attracts writers and artists. Wander round the picturesque streets and browse in the boutiques.

2.00pm

Graves's grave
Take a break for tapas in El Barrigon Xelini (see page 109), a huge and atmospheric bar on the main road, with a pleasant outside terrace. Afterwards visit the poet's simple grave in the hilltop cemetery and his home, Ca N'Alluny, now a small museum.

IN **MALLORCA**

6.00pm

Spectacular sunset
Make your way back down the coast a few kilometres to Son Marroig, home to a 19th-century Austrian archduke who fell in love with the island. You can visit his house and gardens (open until 6.30pm) but the main attraction is the on-site bar from where you can watch the spectacular sunset over Na Foradada.

11.00pm

Nightlife
Back in Palma, take a gentle stroll along the harbour, then, if you have the energy, indulge in a cocktail in the exotic surroundings of Abaco, in Carrer Sant Joan, in the old town.

3.30pm

The beach
Take a 35-minute walk through olive and lemon groves (or opt for a 2km/1-mile drive) to the Cala de Deià, a pretty little rocky cove where you can swim and sunbathe.

8.00pm

A choice of dining
Drive the short distance back the way you came for dinner in one of Deià's excellent restaurants. Go up-market with the modern menu at El Olivo (part of La Residencia hotel), or enjoy excellent home cooking at El Barrigon Xelini (see page 109). Both need advance booking.

CONTENTS

INTRODUCTION

Mallorca could claim to be the perfect holiday island, blessed with attributes that entice millions of foreign visitors annually. The deep blue and translucent turquoise of the Mediterranean, hundreds of kilometres of coastline, secluded rocky coves and wide sandy beaches, a vibrant and sophisticated capital city and some 300 days of brilliant sunshine each year make it irresistible.

A VARIED LANDSCAPE

Lying off the northeast coast of Spain, Mallorca is the largest of the five Balearic Islands, but it is not a big place. It has more than 550km (325 miles) of coastline, but at its widest point – Cap de Sa Mola in the southwest to Capdepera in the northeast – it is only 100km (60 miles) across; at its narrowest, from the Badia d'Alcúdia in the north to the Badia de Palma in the south, it's only half that distance.

The landscape, however, is extremely varied. The dramatic cliffs edging the Serra de Tramuntana, a World Heritage Site, hug the west coast from Andratx all the way to Cap de Formentor. The coastal scenery is stunning, with dizzying drops to the sea and the tiny coves far below and picturesque villages set among centuries-old terraces. To the northwest,

Blue Flag Beaches

Mallorca's beaches didn't always have the sterling reputation they do today. Following a major clean-up campaign, 31 of the 46 Blue Flag beaches in the Balearic Islands belong to Mallorca, a testament to their safety and cleanliness.

Views along the west coast

away from the coast, the Tramuntana range provides ideal walking and climbing conditions. There are 10 main peaks, the highest of which is Puig Major at 1,445 metres (4,741ft). The north coast is dominated by the Bay of Alcúdia – 12km (8 miles) of fine golden sand sloping into shallow waters – and by the grassy wetlands of S'Albufera, now a protected natural park. The interior is a vast plain with sleepy towns, sandstone churches, well-tended farmland, groves of ancient olive trees and orchards of almonds and apricots. On the east coast, long sweeps of beach alternate with intimate little coves and spectacular cave formations, while several picturesque fishing harbours retain their individuality. The south centres on the cosmopolitan capital, Palma, and its splendid bay. Around it, to the east and west, spread the crowded beaches whose glorious sands first brought mass tourism to the island in the late 1950s.

CLIMATE

Mallorca's climate is heavenly for northern Europeans. Although summer extremes of 34°C (93°F) can be uncomfortable, the July–August average is a pleasant 24°C (76°F); winters are mild and not too wet, and even the timid can swim in the sea from June to October.

Magaluf was among the first of the large-scale resorts

VEGETATION AND BIRDLIFE

The flora of the island is as diverse as the landscape. There are cultivated olives, almonds, apricot and citrus trees; holm oaks and pines flourish in mountainous regions, with rosemary, lavender and heather turning the hillsides purple. There are sturdy palm trees growing at sea level, and bougainvillaea brightening village walls; and there are wild orchids and water-loving reeds, sedges and poplars in the S'Albufera marshes.

Mallorca is rich in birdlife. Come in spring, as so many birdwatchers do, to see the numerous migratory birds that come here. The Boquer Valley, near Pollença, is popular with those in the know. S'Albufera, on the north coast, plays host to numerous resident and migrant species, including the cattle egrets that can be seen standing on the backs of cows, pecking insects from their hides, and birds such as Eleonora's falcons, which typically arrive in late spring and hang around until late October/ early November. Among the most colourful and exotic birds that can be seen in many locations in summer are bee-eaters and hoopoes. The island of Cabrera and the Parc Natural de Mondragó in the southeast corner are among the best places to spot migrating seabirds.

THE ISLANDERS AND THEIR LANGUAGE

The population of Mallorca is approximately 895,000, of whom a little less than half – 405,000 – live in the capital. The rest are distributed across 53 municipal districts, with the interior plain being the most sparsely populated region. In the peak summer season, tourists – some 14 million a year, some 60% of whom are German or English – and hordes of seasonal workers, many from Andalusia, swell the population and strain the infrastructure and water supply to their limits.

Mallorcans are bilingual in Spanish and in Mallorquí, a variant of Catalan, which is the official language. Most signs and street names are written in Mallorquí, and this is the language people choose to speak among themselves, and which is used in schools. However, visitors will find locals quite happy to address them in Castilian Spanish, and the high number of seasonal workers from the mainland ensures that Spanish is spoken everywhere.

TOURISM TRENDS

Mallorca was one of the first places in Spain to be developed for tourism in the 1950s. Ever since, it has been one of the major centres, and tourism is now responsible for nearly 90 percent of the island's income. But the industry has had contradictory effects. Income from it made this region Spain's wealthiest per capita, but the environmental and psychological effects of being Europe's low-budget playground have taken a heavy toll. Four decades after it exploded, tourism overheated, leaving a forest of towering hotels and beach-hugging villa communities, whole resorts lined with fast-food outlets, tourist tat shops and loud clubs and bars serving dangerously cheap alcohol. This has led local residents to seek ways to limit so called 'bad tourist activity', including changing how free alcohol is served at all-inclusive resorts and increasing the Sustainable Tourist Tax.

In the 1990s, the island government realised it was time to reassess Mallorca's tourism industry. Fearing that massive over-development and the increasingly bad reputation earned by the raucous behaviour of some visitors, as well as new trends in international tourism, were leaving the Balearics behind, the authorities took action. Moves were made to protect the remaining undeveloped areas as nature preserves, proclaiming them off-limits to construction, and demolishing some of the more unsightly hotel complexes. Almost one third of the island is now under some kind of protection order, and the advantages to the landscape and wildlife are palpable.

There have also been energetic moves to encourage a more up-market and environmentally-friendly kind of tourism. The government's *agroturisme* initiative, which promotes accommodation in small rural hotels and *fincas* (farmhouses) has been extremely popular, both with visitors looking for peace and quiet amid scenic surroundings, and farming families who were struggling to keep their properties going.

Walking paths have been opened up and clearly marked, and a number of hilltop sanctuaries provide rest and respite for walkers; natural parks are widely promoted and user-friendly. Considerable investment has gone into golf courses and marinas to attract higher-income tourists, and luxury resort and boutique hotels are opening up all over the island.

In Palma de Mallorca, guided walking tours encourage visitors to appreciate the city's heritage, while the range and calibre of the capital's museums and cultural centres is impressive.

ENJOYING THE ISLAND

Throughout the island, summer music festivals are held in beautiful historic buildings, attracting internationally known performers, while traditional, local festivals are also being promoted as a way of disseminating the rural culture of the Balearics. There has also

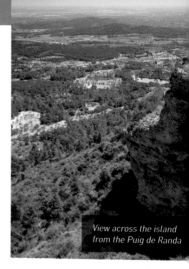

View across the island from the Puig de Randa

been a renewed interest in Mallorcan food, *cuina Mallorquina*, and many venues, from the traditional *cellers* (see page 72) to gourmet restaurants and more basic establishments are experiencing a surge in popularity.

Mallorca is easy to get around. Hiring a car is relatively inexpensive and stress free, as most roads (except the stretch around the Bay of Palma) don't get too busy, even in summer, and parking (outside of the capital) is not a problem. Public transport is good too: there are regular buses from Palma to most points of interest (some services are limited on Sundays), and regular rail service – including the scenic rail journey on the narrow-gauge line to Sóller (see page 54). For another aspect of the island, you can take boat trips along much of the coast.

With all of this going for it, Mallorca is not simply a place for sun, sea and sand holidays – but there is no denying that those are still excellent reasons to come here.

A BRIEF HISTORY

Many influences have shaped Mallorca over the past 4,000 years and helped make it the fascinating place it is today. The stone towers called *talayots* that can still be seen in parts of the island were defensive structures built by early inhabitants, who are believed to have made settlements here around 1300BC. Even before that, Neolithic islanders had graduated from cave dwellings to simple stone houses and cleared fields by piling stones into dividing walls – the origins of the intricate dry-stone walls called *parets seques* or *margers* that can still be seen in the island interior.

Over the centuries, the inhabitants traded with the Phoenicians, Carthaginians and Greeks, and the Carthaginians gradually colonised the islands (c. 400BC), absorbed them into their trading empire and founded the main ports. But by 123BC the Romans, who had pacified most of Spain, despatched an invading force to conquer the islands, which they named Balearis Major (Mallorca) and Balearis Minor (Menorca).

Balearic Slingers

The early inhabitants' skill with stones was evident in their deadly use of the slingshot. The 'Balearic slingers' were renowned throughout the Mediterranean world and recruited by Hannibal to fight for the Carthaginians in the Punic Wars against Rome. The name Balearic probably comes from the Greek word, *ballein*, 'to throw'.

ROMANS, VANDALS AND MOORISH OCCUPATION

The Romans introduced the Christian religion, constructed roads and established the towns of Palmaria (Palma) and Pollentia (near Alcúdia), but during the 5th century AD, as the Roman

The talayotic settlement at Ses Païsses

Empire crumbled, Goths, Vandals and Visigoths poured into the Balearics. The Vandals destroyed almost all evidence of Roman occupation – the remains of Pollentia outside Alcúdia are among the very few traces left – before they were ousted in AD534 by a Byzantine expedition from Constantinople.

But more invaders were to follow. Ignited by the teachings of the Prophet Mohammed, Islam spread quickly in the 8th century. A Moorish army led by General Tarik landed on the Iberian Peninsula in 711 and in just seven years, most of Spain was under Moorish rule. While the Balearics remained submissive, the *caliphs* (rulers) were content to accept tribute from them, but local disturbances prompted an invasion at the beginning of the 10th century. Both islands were conquered and became part of the Caliphate of Córdoba.

Although little Moorish architecture remains – the Arab Baths in Palma and the Jardins d'Alfàbia near Sóller are two

The Banys Àrabs in Palma

exceptions – the influence can be seen in Palma, in the Palau de l'Almudaina, in the fountains in S'Hort del Rei, and in many shady patios. Some place names are also of Arabic origin – Alcúdia (Al-Kudia) means 'on the hill', and Binissalem means 'son of peace'.

THE RECONQUEST

The aim of the crusades in Spain was the eviction of the Muslims. After the recovery of Jerusalem in 1099, it took 400 years of sieges and battles, treaties and betrayals before Christian rulers succeeded in subduing the Moors. In 1229, a Catalan army led by King Jaume I of Aragón and Catalunya took Mallorca. Jaume proved to be an enlightened ruler who profited from the talents of the Moors – those who remained were forcibly converted to Christianity – as well as those of the large Jewish and Genoese trading communities.

Jaume I reigned in Aragón for six decades, but he made the mistake of dividing between his sons the lands he had united. Initially this resulted in the Independent Kingdom of Mallorca, first under Jaume II, then under Sanxo and Jaume III. But dynastic rivalry triggered the overthrow of the latter by his cousin, Pere IV. Attempting to make a comeback, Jaume III was killed in battle near Llucmajor in 1349.

In the following century the Catholic Monarchs, Ferdinand and Isabella, leading a unified Spain, completed the

Reconquest, taking Granada, the only Moorish enclave left on the peninsula, in 1492.

THE SPANISH EMPIRE

As one tumultuous age ended, another began. Christopher Columbus (Cristobal Colón), the seafaring captain from Genoa (whom at least three Mallorcan towns claim as their own), believed he could reach the East Indies by sailing westwards. In the same year that Granada fell, Columbus crossed the Atlantic. Spain exported its adventurers, traders and priests, and imposed its language, culture and religion on the New World, creating a vast empire in the Americas. Ruthless, avaricious conquistadors extracted and sent back incalculable riches in the form of silver and gold. The century and a half after 1492 was known as Spain's Golden Age, but it carried the seeds of its own decline. Plagued by corruption and incompetence, and drained of manpower and ships by such adventurism as the dispatch of the ill-fated Armada against England in 1588, Spain was unable to defend her expansive interests.

The Balearic Islands did not benefit much from Spain's glory years. They were forbidden to trade with the New World, and their existing trade on the eastern routes was interrupted

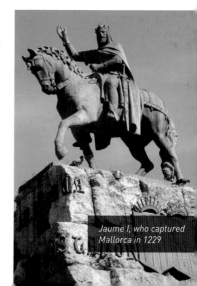

Jaume I, who captured Mallorca in 1229

Ferdinand and Isabella greet Christopher Columbus

by marauding pirates based in North Africa, as well as by the powerful Turkish fleet.

WARS AND CONSEQUENCES

The daughter of Ferdinand and Isabella married the heir to the Holy Roman Emperor, Maximilian of Habsburg. The Spanish crown duly passed to the Habsburgs and remained in their hands until the feeble-minded Carlos II died in 1700, leaving no heir. France seized the chance to install the young grandson of Louis XIV on the Spanish throne. A rival Habsburg claimant was supported by Austria and Britain, who saw a powerful Spanish-French alliance as a major threat. In the subsequent War of the Spanish Succession (1702–13) most of the kingdom of Aragón, including the Balearics, backed the Habsburgs. Britain seized Menorca and retained it, under the Treaty of Utrecht, when the war was over.

By 1805, Spain was once more aligned with France, and Spanish ships fought alongside the French against Admiral Lord Nelson at the Battle of Trafalgar. But Napoleon came to distrust his Spanish ally and forcibly replaced the king of Spain with his own brother, Joseph Bonaparte. A French army marched in to subdue the country. The Spanish resisted and, aided by British troops commanded by the Duke of Wellington, drove the French out. What the British call the Peninsular War (1808–14) is known in Spain as the War of Independence.

During the 19th century, most of Spain's possessions in the Americas broke away. The Balearics, further neglected, were beset with poverty and thousands of islanders emigrated to South America in search of a better life. A brief upturn, due to the successful trade in wine, ended when the phylloxera louse destroyed the island's vines.

CRISES, REPUBLIC AND CIVIL WAR

The beginning of the 20th century in Spain was marked by social and political crises, assassinations and near anarchy. The colonial war in Morocco provided a distraction, but a disastrous defeat there in 1921 led to a coup and the dictatorship of General Primo de Rivera. He fell in 1929, and when elections of 1931 revealed massive anti-royalist feeling, the king followed him into exile.

The new republic was conceived amid an outbreak of strikes and uprisings. In February 1936 the left-wing Popular Front won a majority of seats in the Cortes (parliament), but across Spain localised violence displaced debate. In July 1936,

⊙ CREATIVE INPUT

Mallorca has always attracted creative people. In 1838 Frédéric Chopin and George Sand spent several months in Valldemossa, during which he composed *The Raindrop Prelude* and she wrote *A Winter in Majorca*. Poet and author Robert Graves came to Deià in 1929 and made it his home; he is buried in the little churchyard on the hill. Agatha Christie stayed at Hotel Illa d'Or in Port de Pollença in 1932, which inspired her novel *Problems at Pollensa Bay*. Artist Joan Miró, whose wife Pilar was Mallorcan, set up a house and studio in Palma in 1956, rather than live under the Franco regime and he, too, stayed until his death (in 1983).

General Francisco Franco staged a coup, which was supported by the military, monarchists, conservatives, the clergy and the right-wing Falangist movement. Aligned on the Republican government's side were liberals, socialists, communists and anarchists. The ensuing Spanish Civil War (1936–39) was brutal and bitter. Support for both sides poured in from outside Spain. Those on the Republican side believed it was a contest between democracy and dictatorship, while Nationalist supporters saw it as a battle between order and communist chaos. During the three years the war lasted, around one million Spaniards lost their lives.

Mallorca and Menorca found themselves on opposite sides. Menorca declared for the Republic, and stayed with it to the bitter end. Mallorca's garrison seized the island for the Nationalists. A decisive factor was the presence in Palma of Italian air squadrons, used to bomb Republican Barcelona.

NEW HORIZONS

Exhausted after the Civil War, Spain remained on the sidelines during World War II and, after the dark years of isolation known as the Noche Negra (Black Night), began a slow economic recovery under Franco's oppressive, law-and-order regime, boosted by the growth of the tourism industry.

A small élite had visited the island in the 1920s, but it was in the late 1950s and early 1960s that northern Europeans first began making sun-seeking pilgrimages to Spain, and the Balearic Islands, in any numbers. Tourism transformed the impoverished country's economy, landscape and society. Eager to capitalise, government and private interests poured everything into mass tourism, triggering a rash of uncontrolled and indiscriminate building, with scant regard for tradition or aesthetics. Almost as influential as the financial input was the injection of foreign influences, particularly those associated with the liberalism of the 1960s.

Mallorca, once dependent on agriculture, fishing and small local industries, experienced an explosive growth in tourism and swiftly became one of Europe's most popular holiday destinations.

After the death of General Franco in 1975, his designated successor, the grandson of Alfonso XIII, was crowned King Juan Carlos I. The king managed a smooth transition to democracy, then stood back to allow it full rein. After decades of repression, new freedoms and autonomy were granted to the Spanish regions and their languages and cultures enjoyed a long-sought renaissance. The Balearic Islands won a degree of autonomy in 1978 and five years later became the

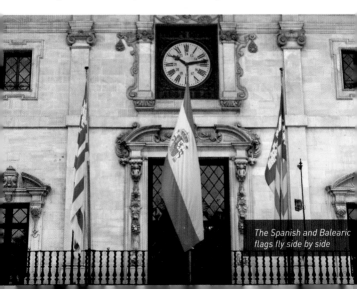

The Spanish and Balearic flags fly side by side

Comunidad Autónoma de las Islas Baleares. Mallorquí was recognised officially as the language of Mallorca.

MODERNISATION

Spain joined the European Community (now the European Union) in 1986, which gave a further boost to an expanding economy. Mallorca's tourist industry continued to grow but so did a realisation that lack of planning and good taste were leading to damaging long-term consequences – to the environment and to the island's reputation. By the late 1990s, when the lager lout image had become too closely associated with some resorts, production of domestic waste was double the national average and electricity consumption had increased by 37 percent in five years, a new emphasis on quality tourism and safeguarding the environment had taken root. Building restrictions were implemented and a substantial number of areas were declared protected zones.

The economic crisis in 2008 initially saw a downturn in visitor numbers, but since then things have picked up considerably, with Mallorca (along with the other Balearic Islands, Ibiza and Menorca) being one of the top tourist destinations in the European Union. In 2013, Palma's Pier Ponent was extended to accommodate large cruise ships and the airport was also enlarged to cope with the increasing number of visitors from outside the EU. Recent years have been marred by the growing opposition to mass tourism as well as discontent with the high unemployment rate among the younger population.

In 2016, the Sustainable Tourism Tax was implemented in an effort to fund more sustainable tourism and further protect the island. And in 2020, alcohol limits will come into effect at bars in certain areas and at all-inclusive hotels.

HISTORICAL LANDMARKS

c. 1300BC Megalithic Talayotic culture; stone towers, *talayots*, built.

c. 400BC Carthaginians colonise the Balearics.

123BC–AD400 Romans invade; they name the island Balearis Major and establish towns such as Palmaria (Palma) and Pollentia (Alcúdia).

711 Moors land near Gibraltar, and Spain falls under Islamic rule.

848 Moorish rule imposed in the Balearics; it lasts for 300 years.

1229 Mallorca taken by the Christian army under Jaume I.

1285–87 Alfonso III of Aragón captures Palma.

1349 Jaume III killed in battle by Pere IV of Aragón, ending the Independent Kingdom of Mallorca.

1492 Spain united under the Catholic Monarchs.

1837 First steamship service links Mallorca and Spanish mainland.

1936–39 Spanish Civil War. Mallorca seized by Nationalist forces.

1936–75 Franco's dictatorship; economic hardship in the early years.

1960 Mallorca's airport built. Tourism begins to replace agriculture as the island's main source of income.

1975 Juan Carlos I becomes king after the death of Franco.

1978 Statute of Autonomy gives the Balearic Islands a degree of autonomy; five years later they become an autonomous province and Catalan/Mallorquí is restored as the official language.

1986 Spain joins the European Community (now European Union).

1996 The government of the Balearic Islands initiates measures to protect the environment and encourage eco-friendly tourism.

2016 A new Tax for Sustainable Tourism more commonly known as the 'tourist tax' is introduced for tourist accommodations on the island.

2017 Mallorca passes a law that makes it illegal for bulls to perform for more than 10 minutes or to use sharp implements or have horses in the ring. This makes the sport nearly impossible to stage.

2018 Massive flooding across the eastern part of the island kills at least 10 people.

2020 New rules as to how alcohol is served at bars in certain areas and at all-inclusive hotels comes into effect.

Sant Elm, with the island of Sa Dragonera

WHERE TO GO

Although some visitors to this small Mediterranean island arrive by ferry from mainland Spain, the majority land at Palma's airport, Son Sant Joan, 9km (5.5 miles) outside the capital, Palma de Mallorca. A ring road – the Via Cintura – skirts the city, with roads radiating off to the rest of the island; to the craggy, beautiful northwest coast, the quiet, friendly towns of the interior plain, the wetlands of S'Albufera in the north, the tiny calas in the east, and the tourist-dominated strips to the east and west of Palma and along the north coast.

Tour agencies offer excursions, by coach or boat, or a combination of the two, to hidden beaches, mountain villages, spectacular caves and weekly markets, but hiring a car (see page 117) is the best way to get around. The railway options are currently rather limited – the T1 goes to Inca, while the T2 continues to Sa Pobla in the north and the T3 goes to Manacor in the east. There is also the tourist railway which takes passengers along the picturesque route to Sóller. New railway lines are in progress and expected for completion by 2026. Bus service throughout Mallorca is comprehensive and reliable (see page 131).

PALMA DE MALLORCA

Set around a sheltered bay, **Palma ❶** is a large, cosmopolitan city, with around 405,000 inhabitants – nearly half the permanent population of Mallorca. It is very much a Mediterranean city, with palm trees and bushes of fragrant oleander, outdoor cafés with colourful awnings, and yachts and working vessels bobbing in the bay alongside one another. Palma is a city with a long history, as the Gothic cathedral towering above the city

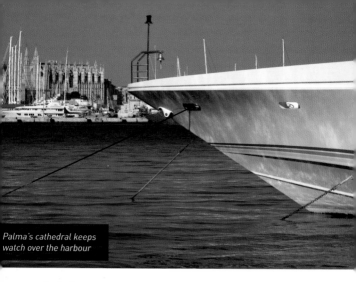

Palma's cathedral keeps watch over the harbour

walls indicates as you approach from the airport. It's smart and urbane, with designer boutiques, smart restaurants and chic art galleries hidden in narrow alleys. Come sundown, it's a lively city that stays awake long into the night too.

The old quarter surrounding the cathedral – 'Centre Historic' on direction signs – sits on a small hill overlooking the bay, and its narrow, atmospheric streets are full of pleasant surprises. To the east of the centre is the Platja de Palma, a long line of excellent sandy beaches that have been defaced by a stretch of concrete from Ca'n Pastilla to S'Arenal. To the west is the seaside promenade of modern Palma, where luxury hotels look out over a forest of masts in the yacht harbour, although divided from it by a stretch of six-lane highway. Crowning the wooded slopes above the city, where the Spanish royal family have a summer home, are the stone towers of the Castell de Bellver (see page 41).

THE CATHEDRAL

Standing proudly above the city walls, spectacular when illuminated at night, is the **Cathedral** Ⓐ (www.catedralde-mallorca.org; Apr–May Mon–Fri 10am–5.15pm, June–Sept Mon–Fri 10am–6.15pm, Nov–Mar Mon–Fri 10am–3.15pm, Sat year round 10am–2.15pm; entered via the museum). Also known as **La Seu**, this is one of the finest Gothic churches in the whole of Spain. Begun in 1230 by Jaume I, on the site of the Great Mosque after the Christians recaptured the island from the Moors, it took nearly four centuries to complete. Densely packed flying buttresses on the south front create an extraordinary effect, especially in the glow of the setting sun, when they are reflected in the lake of the Parc de la Mar below.

The 14th-century **Portal del Mirador** on this same front is a feast of carved stone figurines by architect and sculptor Guillem Sagrera (1397–1454), including a depiction of *The Last Supper*. Entry via the Portal de l'Almoina, below the square, 13th-century bell tower, is reserved for those attending mass. Before you go in, stop to admire the splendid view of the Bay of Palma from the **Mirador** to the south.

The **Museu del Catedral** (hours as above) contains a splendid silver monstrance, some interesting medieval

Cathedral tower by night

paintings and holy relics. Sections of the original Roman city can be seen through a glass floor. An early Renaissance doorway in carved stone leads into the baroque Chapter House. The vault of the cathedral's three-aisled, 121m (396ft) interior is supported by slim, elegant pillars. The largest of the seven **rose windows** is magnificent, 12m (40ft) across, composed of 1,236 separate sections of stained glass. The extraordinary *baldachino*, a wrought-iron crown of thorns over the high altar, was added by Catalan *Moderniste* architect Antoni Gaudí, creator of Barcelona's Sagrada Família, who worked for 10 years on the cathedral in the early 20th century. (*Modernisme* is the Catalan version of Art Nouveau.) The tombs of Jaume II and Jaume III, 14th-century kings of Catalunya and Mallorca, are in the Capella de la Trinitá at the east end. And St Peter's chapel is covered with innovative ceramics by Mallorcan artist Miquel Barceló, on which he worked for six years before it was unveiled in February 2007.

To the east of the Cathedral is the **Museu Diocesà** (the same hours as the cathedral), back in its permanent home in the Episcopal Palace. It contains medieval and Gothic statuary along with some lovely stained-glass windows by Gaudí, who lived in the palace while he worked on the Cathedral. The palace itself is well worth a look, too.

Guided Tours

In summer, a number of guided tours cover aspects such as Modernisme, the Jewish Quarter, the patios, a night tour, and one called Palma Monumental that gives a good historical background. Pick up leaflets from one of the tourist offices, or contact tel: 902 102 365.

PALAU DE L'ALMUDAINA

The **Palau de l'Almudaina** Ⓑ (Tue–Sun Apr–Sept 10am–8pm, Oct–Mar until 6pm; free to EU citizens summer Wed–Thu 5–8pm, winter 3–5pm; www.patrimonionacional.

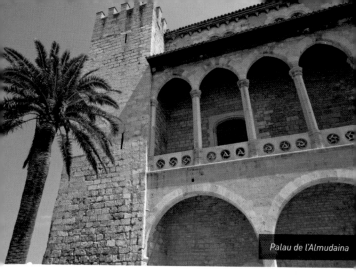

Palau de l'Almudaina

es) stands just opposite of the cathedral. Once the residence of the Moorish vizirs, then of the medieval kings of Mallorca, it is a perfect blend of Islamic and Catalan-Gothic architecture. There is a stone-vaulted, 13th-century throne room (the Tinell), a pretty courtyard (Patio del Rei), a Gothic chapel (Capella de Santa Anna), and heavily restored royal offices, sometimes used by the present king, where traces of early paintwork survive on the ceilings and walls. There are also some impressive 15th- and 16th-century Flemish tapestries.

AROUND THE HISTORIC CENTRE

In Carrer Palau Reial, to the north of the Almudaina, where brightly painted horse-drawn carriages wait for customers (when a heat alert is in place they are forbidden from working between noon and 5pm), is another palace, which houses the **Palau March Museu** ● (www.fundacionbmarch.es; Mon–Fri

Apr–Oct 10am–6.30pm, Nov–Mar 10am–5pm, Sat 10am–2pm). Within this majestic building and its courtyard a small but superb collection of contemporary sculpture has been gathered, including works by Henry Moore, Barbara Hepworth, Rodin and Chillida, and murals by the Catalan artist Josep Maria Sert, as well as high-quality temporary exhibitions. The palace is also a venue for classical concerts in spring and summer.

The ochre colonnades of the Parliament Building – **Parlament de les Illes Baleares** – run along nearly the full length of Carrer Palau Reial. At the far end, the opulent Renaissance facade of the **Ajuntament** (Town Hall), its overhanging wooden roof supported by carved beams, dominates the **Plaça del Cort**. (You can go inside to see the huge processional figures that are stored here; www.palma.cat; Sun 11am and noon, guided tours in English by appointment only, booking essential tel: 618 914 517 or email visites@palma.cat) In the centre of the square is an ancient, gnarled olive tree, a favourite spot for photos.

Turn right from the *plaça* and you will reach a pleasant little square, named for the 14th-century church of **Santa Eulàlia** **D**, which has a Gothic nave, altar paintings by Francisco Gomez and several baroque chapels. Behind the church in the narrow Carrer Can Sanç (off Carrer Carnisseria) is **Can Joan de S'Aigo** (http://canjoandesaigo.com; daily 8am–9pm), a beautifully tiled café, founded in 1700, which was artist Joan Miró's favourite place for hot chocolate and almond cake, and popular with everyone for ice-cream.

A right turn brings you to Plaça Quadrado, shaded by palms and plane trees, and with a number of attractive *Moderniste* buildings, the best one being Can Barceló (1902). Above the third-storey oriel windows the facade is decorated with mosaics portraying domestic scenes with women and children. The massive 13th-century **Basílica de Sant Francesc** **E** (Mon–Sat

9.30am–12.30pm and 3.10pm–6pm, Sun and bank holidays 9am–noon) backs onto Quadrado, and dominates the adjoining Plaça Sant Francesc. A sculpture outside depicts Mallorcan missionary Fray Juníper Serra, founder of the first Californian missions (see page 70). To the left of the baroque altar a chapel contains the alabaster tomb of Catalan scholar, mystic and missionary Ramón Llull

Basilica de Sant Francesc

(1235–1316). But the main event is the enchanting Gothic cloister (through which you enter the church), with slender columns, delicate tracery and lemon trees around a central fountain.

PATIOS AND MUSEUMS

The old quarter of Palma is rich in baronial mansions, most dating from the 16th–18th centuries, with wonderful patios behind their great wooden doors. With ornate staircases, decorated tiles, palms and potted plants, sometimes cooled by small fountains, they are a delight. Among the best are Can Olesa on Carrer Morey, Can Tacón on Carrer de Sant Jaume II, and Can Bordils (Palma Municipal Archive) and Can Oms, both on Carrer Almudaina.

Most are private or commercial properties and you have to be content with peeping through the gateways. Alternatively, you can see several of these patios by visiting the museums housed within. On Carrer de la Portella, the renovated Renaissance **Ca**

Inside Can Marquès

La Gran Cristiana houses the **Museu de Mallorca** (http://museudemallorca. caib.es; Mon–Fri 10am– 6pm, Sat–Sun 11am–2pm). Exhibits include 13th- to 16th-century religious paintings, *Moderniste* tiles and 20th-century paint-ings. The prehistory and classical archaeology rooms were undergoing refurbishment at the time of writing.

Another splendid man-sion with a patio in Carrer de la Portella is the **Can Morey de Santmartí** that used to be the home and studio of the 20th-century Catalan portraitist and landscape painter Xim Torrens Lladó.

The former private mansion Can Marquès on Carrer Apuntadors is now the newly renovated five-star hotel **Palacio Can Marquès**. Originally 15th-century, the house was mostly furnished and decorated in bourgeois, 19th-century style, with some interesting *Moderniste* additions. Following careful renovation it has been converted into 13 unique and luxurious suites, with the interiors designed by New York-based Aline Matsika.

Not far away, on Carrer Can Serra, are the **Banys Àrabs** ❻ (Arab Baths; daily 10am–5.30pm), still standing after 1,000 years. The courtyard garden is a tranquil, beautiful place when it's not filled with excursion groups. Late afternoon is a good time to go.

MODERNISTE SITES

Alternatively, retrace your steps to Plaça Cort, from where it is only a short walk up the intriguing little shopping streets of Carrer Colom and Jaume II to the deep yellow facades and green shutters of the former market place, the **Plaça Major** Ⓖ. The square is busy with cafés, street entertainers and handicraft stalls selling scarves, jewellery and batik work. Escalators lead down to a subterranean shopping mall and public toilets.

Approaching the square, you pass the **Plaça Marquès del Palmer** where there are two excellent examples of *Moderniste* architecture – Can Forteza Rei and L'Àguila, adorned with ornate iron grillwork and colourful ceramic flourishes; a café and a smart shoe shop occupy the ground floors.

Down a flight of steps from the Plaça Major, lined with tourist-trap kiosks, is Plaça Weyler, with two more fine examples of *Modernisme*. The major one is the imposing **Gran Hotel** Ⓗ, now run as a cultural centre by the **Fundació La Caixa** (www.obrasociallacaixa.org; Tue–Sat 10am–8pm, Sun 11am–2pm). It includes a bookshop, a smart café/restaurant and an art centre that stages excellent exhibitions of contemporary art – home-grown and international – and has a permanent display of the work of Catalan

Gran Hotel

The Forn des Teatre

painter Hermen Anglada Camarasa (1872–1959), who lived in Pollença. This was the first modern hotel in Mallorca, built in 1903 by Lluís Doménech i Muntaner. Following a chequered history, La Caixa (Spain's third largest financial institution) acquired it in 1987 and, after renovation works, reopened in 1993.

Across from the Gran Hotel is a small bakery and café, the **Forn des Teatre** (www.fornetdelasoca. com), whose graceful facade graces many a postcard. Down the street, on Plaça Mercat, stand the two gently undulating *Moderniste* buildings that comprise **Can Casasayas**. The bakery got its name from the neighbouring **Teatre Principal**, a grand edifice that stages plays, operas and concerts (see page 93). Follow the road past the theatre and you reach **Via Roma**, an avenue called La Rambla after Barcelona's promenade.

BARRÍ SANT MIQUEL

Turn right from Plaça Major, instead of descending the steps, and you will be in Carrer Sant Miquel, a busy pedestrianised shopping street, where the **Museu Fundació Joan March ❶** (www.march.es/arte/palma; Mon–Fri 10am–6.30pm, Sat 10.30am–2pm; guided tours available; free) is located. This striking 18th-century building, with marble staircases and good stained glass, houses an exceptional collection belonging to the wealthy March banking family. The 70-strong permanent collection includes works by Picasso, Miró, Dalí, Tàpies and Juan Gris.

Heading north up the street you will come to the church of **Sant Miquel** (Mon–Sat 8am–13.30pm, 5pm–7.30pm, Sun 10am–12.30pm, 6pm–7.30pm), where the first Mass after the Christian reconquest was celebrated. This ancient church is the religious heart of the neighbourhood, a solid building with a fine baroque altarpiece. A little further on is the deconsecrated church of **Sant Antoniet**, whose pretty courtyard plays host to a variety of temporary art exhibitions (Mon–Fri 10am–2pm, 3.30pm–8pm, Sat 10am–1.30pm) and the walls and pavement outside have become an informal gallery space for local amateur artists.

Round the corner, on the right, is the **Mercat de l'Olivar ❶** (www.mercatolivar.com; Mon–Thu, 7am–2.30pm, Fri

⊘ THE MARCH DYNASTY

The Fundació March was set up by the extremely wealthy March banking dynasty in 1955 as a philanthropic institution to promote science and culture. You will see branches of the Banca March all over the Balearic Islands, and notice their name appended to numerous cultural ventures. As well as the two major museums mentioned here, there is an extensive library and archive in the Palau March, open to the public as well, and concerts are held there in summer. The foundation also funds an annual programme of 20th-century classical music at Palma's Auditorio and summer concerts in the Jardins March in Cala Ratjada, where there is some splendid modern sculpture. Annual prizes for literary criticism and short novels are also awarded by a dynasty that obviously believes in putting a lot back into the community on which its wealth was founded.

7am–8pm, Sat 7am–3pm), the city's largest fish, meat and produce market. A very short distance further along Carrer Caputxins is the Plaça d'Espanya, where you will find the new Estació Intermodal, the combined rail, metro and bus station.

PASSEIG DES BORN TO THE WATERFRONT

If you go west instead of north from Plaça Weyler, along traffic-filled Carrer Unió, you come to Plaça Rei Joan Carles I. Ahead is the busy shopping street, Avinguda Jaume III; to your left, the leafy **Passeig des Born**. The broad central avenue, lined with benches and guarded at either end by stone sphinxes, runs down to **Plaça de la Reina** 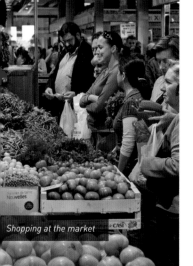, with a large central fountain. At No. 27, the elegant 18th-century **Palau Solleric** (http://casalsolleric.palma.cat; Tue–Sat 11am–2pm, 3.30pm–8.30pm, Sun 11am–2.30pm; free) houses a cultural foundation, hosts contemporary art exhibitions and has a café and a tourist information desk.

To the left of Plaça de la Reina (past the tourist office) steps lead up to the cathedral, where we began. Hugging the old city walls is **S'Hort del Rei**, a lovely Arabic-style garden, with fountains and pools, which makes a pleasant distraction from city traffic. Miró's beloved **Personatge** sculpture *The Egg* stands on the corner nearest the *plaça*. Facing it is the cool

Shopping at the market

and minimalist café that is part of the Palau March. Parallel to S'Hort del Rei, a much-needed car park was constructed beneath a stretch of the Avinguda Antoni Maura. Below the city walls, on the southern side, the attractively landscaped **Parc de la Mar** forms a barrier against the coastal motorway, the **Passeig Marítim**. The park has an artificial lake and modern sculpture, including works by Miró, and is

Miró's Personatge sculpture

the venue for free open-air concerts on summer evenings, as is Ses Voltes, lying directly beneath the Cathedral walls.

A right turn here leads to the turreted **Sa Llotja ⑬** (www.palma.cat; open only if there are exhibitions; free) in the square of the same name. Designed in the 15th century by Guillem Sagrera (after whom this stretch of the Passeig Marítim is named), it was once the merchants' stock exchange, and is one of Spain's finest civic Gothic buildings, with slim columns twisting through a light and airy interior to the vaulted roof. It is now used for art exhibitions. Nearby **Plaça Drassana** is a pleasant if somewhat shabby neighbourhood square. Here, the 17th-century **Consolat de Mar**, the former maritime law court, is the HQ of the president of the Balearic Islands' government. The two buildings are linked by the Porta del Mar, one of the old city gates. The maze of narrow streets between Plaça de Sa Llotja and Plaça de la Reina form Palma's lively restaurant and nightlife area.

Cross the road at the nearest traffic lights to explore Palma's harbour and waterfront, in all its diversity. You will probably spot some anglers mending their nets (although the fishing fleet is not what it was), smart yachts around the **Real Club Náutic** (www.rcnp.es), a tiny fishermen's chapel, Sant Elm, opportunities to take trips around the harbour, and, at the western end, the ferry passenger terminal. En route, several pleasant cafés and restaurants overlook the port, while cyclists, runners and roller-bladers whizz past on a designated track. The harbour front is planted with palms, hibiscus and oleander, but there is no ignoring the fact that six lanes of traffic are roaring past on the other side. Despite this, it is very pleasant on a summer evening, when the sun is setting over the water and there's a great view of the illuminated cathedral.

Almost opposite the Real Club Náutic is the prestigious **Es Baluard Museu d'Art Modern i Contemporani** Ⓜ (www.esbaluard. org; Tue–Sat 10am–8pm, Sun 10am–3pm), housed in a stunning white structure built into the city fortifications in Plaça Porta de Santa Catalina. Their temporary exhibitions change regularly and are a fascinating reason to visit, but they also have works by Picasso, Miró and Tàpies as well as Mallorcan artists Miquel Barceló and Juli Ramis on display. The views of the port and the city from the museum's rooftop and terrace are impressive. Classical music recitals are held in the museum on some evenings.

OUT-OF-TOWN ATTRACTIONS

Further west there are three more places worth mentioning. The **Poble Espanyol** Ⓝ (www.puebloespanolmallorca.com; Nov–Mar 9am–5pm, Apr–Oct 10am–6pm), a walled town of replica architectural treasures from across Spain, is kitsch but entertaining. The buildings house shops, craft studios, bars and cafés. It is reached on foot (20 minutes from the city centre) or by bus Nos. 5, 29, 46 (Adrea Doria bus stop) and 50 (Bus Turistic).

Just south of the Poble Espanyol, perched on a hilltop, is **Castell de Bellver** 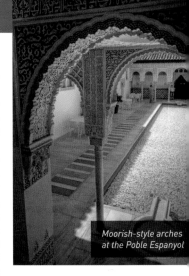 (http://castell-debellver.palma.cat; Apr–Sept Tue–Sat until 7pm, Sun 10am–3pm, Oct–Mar Tue–Sat 10am–6pm, Sun 10am–3pm; free on Sundays; guided tours in English Tue–Sat at 11am; a minimum of five persons is required), reached on bus Nos 3, 20, 46 and 50. A magnificent example of Gothic military architecture, the castle has commanded the approaches to the city since the 14th century. From the battlements, the view of the city and the bay is quite stunning. Inside, the small **Museu d'Història de la Ciutat** traces the history and archaeology of the area.

Moorish-style arches at the Poble Espanyol

The best of the three is the **Fundació Pilar i Joan Miró** (https://miromallorca.com; Tue–Sat mid-May–mid-Sept 10am–7pm, mid-Sept–mid-May 10am–6pm, Sun 10am–3pm all year; free on Saturdays between 3pm–6pm and first Sun of each month) in Carrer Joan de Saridakis in the suburb of Cala Major. Bus No. 3, 20, or 46 will take you right to the door, but a taxi from the centre is not too expensive. The Catalan artist and his Mallorcan wife lived on the island, from 1956 until his death in 1983, and the foundation displays a fine selection of his work.

THE WESTERN CORNER

When tourism hit Mallorca, the Bay of Palma, with two magnificent sweeps of white sand almost 30km (18 miles) long, was irresistible, and the resorts that mushroomed along here in the 1960s and 1970s gave the island a name for cheap and cheerful holidays. The picture soon turned decidedly tacky, dominated by down-market tourism and high-rise hotels.

To the west of the bay, things start to improve after Camp de Mar, where the coast road winds through forest to Port d'Andratx. After a detour to Sant Elm, at the island's southwestern tip, there is a beautiful winding coast road to the village of Banyalbufar. Then head inland via the La Granja estate and La Reserva Puig de Galatzó, after which you can complete the circle back to Palma, or carry on up the picturesque west coast. For the southern end of the bay, see page 81.

WEST OF THE BAY

Labyrinth of Lanes

Even disreputable Magaluf has been going upmarket. Exclusive private beach club Nikki Beach (tel: 971 123 962, https://mallorca.nikkibeach.com) has opened here along with some luxury hotels from Meliá including the Sol Wave House (tel: 912 764 747, www.melia.es), which has surf machines and DJs on the terrace.

You can either take the **Via Cintura** (ring road Ma-20), which becomes the Ma-1 motorway at Porto Pi, or the coast road. Either way, you will see a turn-off to **Cala Major** (where the Spanish royal family have their summer home). The coast road runs through the resorts of **Sant Agustí**, with a small yacht harbour, and crowded **Ses Illetes**, to a rocky stretch of coast and the exclusive

Bendinat and **Portals Nous**. Here, apartments cluster on the slopes and a glamorous marina, **Puerto Portals**, has been carved out of the cliffs. All very classy.

Sandy beaches start again at the resorts of **Costa d'En Blanes** – where the popular aquarium, **Marineland**, is situated – and **Palma Nova**. The latter blends almost impercepti-bly into big, brash **Magaluf**. The wide, sandy beach features a solid block of

Portals Vells

bronzing bodies by day; the town centre an equally solid stretch of drinkers by night. This is tourism overkill: vast bars and discos, waterparks, restaurants offering frankfurters, curry and all-day English breakfasts, wide-screen televised football and some of the trashiest shops imaginable. Recent years have seen signifi-cant pushback on some of the area's unchecked tourism and overly rowdy partygoers.

A road lined by pines runs south to the pretty cove of **Portals Vells ❷**, which has somehow escaped much development. In the cliffs are huge caverns dating from Roman times, enlarged over the centuries. Boats make the short excursion from the pier at Magaluf, so it's not always peaceful. Its neighbour, El Mago, was Mallorca's first nudist beach. Not far south of Portals Vells, you can walk to the tranquil cove of **Cala Figuera** (one of three coves on the island with this name), but the end of the peninsula is an abandoned military base that is almost

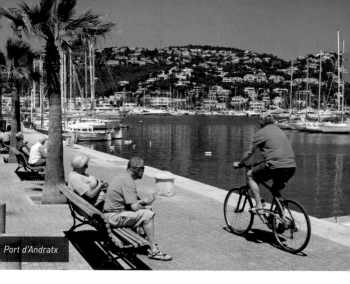

Port d'Andratx

entirely covered with graffiti. Discussions are ongoing about whether to demolish it.

PORT D'ANDRATX AND SANT ELM

Back at Magaluf, pick up the motorway and turn off at Camp de Mar, where a scenic road twists through pine forest to **Port d'Andratx** ❸. More yachts than fishing boats bob on the calm waters of the bay these days. The old harbour area still looks traditional but a string of chic restaurants and shops lines it, and villas and apartments climb the slopes across the water. The lack of a sandy beach has kept the big hotels and package tours away, however, and Port d'Andratx feels relaxed.

The quiet inland town of Andratx plays host to the impressive **Centro Cultural Andratx** (www.ccandratx.com; Mar–Oct Tue–Fri 10.30am–7pm, Sat–Sun 10.30am–4pm, Nov–Feb Tue–Sun 10.30am–4pm), established by a Danish couple, which stages contemporary art exhibitions and runs artists' workshops. This is the largest contemporary art centre in Mallorca. From here you could make a detour to **Sant Elm** ❹, the island's westernmost point, a former fishing village that has retained its identity, though sailors, surfers and divers have known about it for a long time. Offshore, the nature-reserve island of **Sa Dragonera** can be visited almost every day by boat. Check their website (www.conselldemallorca.cat/dragonera) for details about boat operators and routes around the island.

UP THE SCENIC COAST

From Andratx the Ma-10 runs across the southern reaches of the **Serra de Tramuntana**, around numerous hairpin bends to the coast, where it winds along the cliff tops. To the right are terraces planted with fruit trees and olives and some delightful little villages. Along the road stands a succession of *miradors*, lookout points with commanding views of the entire coast, still crowned with ancient watchtowers from which lookouts once scanned the sea for pirate ships. The **Mirador de Ricardo Roca** ❺ has fantastic views of the coast, and a huge restaurant in which to sit and enjoy them.

Estellencs, some 4km (2.5 miles) on, is an ancient village, set amid orange groves on the slopes of Puig de Galatzó (1,027m/3,370ft). From the town you can walk or drive down a track to a little fishing cove. Another 5km (3 miles) further on, one of the finest views of the coast can be had from the 16th-century tower of the **Mirador de Ses Ànimes**. The next town, **Banyalbufar** ❻, is a pretty place with Moorish origins. The Arabic name means 'vineyard by the sea', and it is still famous for its terraced hillsides, a popular haunt for artists. There are a couple of pleasant hotels, several restaurants, and a lane twists down to a rocky cove whose crystal-clear water is ideal for diving.

The manor house at La Granja

LA GRANJA

North of Banyalbufar, the road turns inland, in the direction of **Esporles**, close to which you'll find the estate of **La Granja** ❼ (www.lagranja.net; daily 10am–7pm, winter until 6pm). It is a bit of a theme park, but still worth a visit. In Roman times the estate was renowned for the purity of its water, and there are still numerous fountains in the leafy gardens. The interior of the house is magnificent and gives a good idea of how the landed classes once lived. The chapel and the torture chamber speak for themselves. The donkeys, pigs, wild goats and sheep in the grounds are usually a hit with children; you might even witness a black vulture soaring overhead, too. There are tastings of fig bread and local cheese and sausages. From Feb–Oct, there is a craft and horse show on Wed and Fri at 4pm, while Thursdays have performances of regional music, folk dancing and dressage at 4pm.

From here, you can return to Palma on the Ma-1120, continue up the west coast, or take the minor road to Puigpunyent to visit **La Reserva Puig de Galatzó** ❽ (www.lareservamallorca.com; daily 10am–6pm; last admittance 2 hours before closing). Some 3km (2 miles) of paths run past waterfalls and caves through protected land, rich in bird and animal life, on the lush slopes of Galatzó, known as the mystical mountain because of its magnetic properties. The paths are fairly easy, although you need sensible shoes. If you want something more adventurous you can try abseiling, climbing, mountain biking, zip lining and crossing rope bridges – although these so-called 'Adventure Trails' are quite expensive.

THE WEST COAST

This is one of the most dramatic and beautiful routes in Mallorca. It's hard to pick a highlight as there are so many, from Valldemossa, where George Sand and Frédéric Chopin once stayed, to the lovely hilltop village of Deià, once home to poet Robert Graves, the cliff-top mansion of the Habsburg Archduke Ludwig, and the agreeable town of Sóller.

Whether you are continuing a route round the coast on the Ma-10 or coming

Valldemossa monastery

Chopin's death mask, amongst memorabilia at the monastery

direct from Palma on the Ma-1110, a good, relatively straight road, running through groves of olives and almonds, your first stop will be at Valldemossa. As you approach, the incline becomes steeper and the village and monastery suddenly appear, like something out of a fairy tale.

LA REAL CARTUJA DE VALLDEMOSSA

Although **Valldemossa** ❾ was the birthplace of Mallorca's only home-grown saint, Catalina Tomás, it was the visit, in the winter of 1838–39, of French writer George Sand – Armandine Dupin-Dudevant – and her lover, Frédéric Chopin, that really put the town on the map. They don't seem to have been very happy here; Chopin was unwell, the weather was miserable, and the villagers disapproved of Sand's habit of wearing men's clothes and smoking cigars. She disparaged the local people in her book, *A Winter in Majorca*, calling them 'barbarians and thieves', although she thought Mallorca 'the most beautiful place I have ever lived'.

Nowadays, coach loads of visitors disturb the peace of this little hilltop town as they come to see the couple's lodgings in the former Carthusian monastery, **La Real Cartuja de Valldemossa** (www.cartoixadevalldemossa.com; Mon–Sat from 10am–4.30pm, closed Nov–Jan). The monastery was founded in 1399, but when the monks were expelled in 1835 some of their cells were sold as apartments – although the 'cells' were three-room suites with private gardens. Those rented by Sand and Chopin are now a museum, which displays manuscripts, Chopin's death mask and his piano. You can also visit the massive church, the pharmacy, with a beautiful collection of 18th-century ceramic jars, the library and the Prior's Cell, complete with a life-size model of a prior. There is an interesting **Museu Municipal** here, too, with documents relating to the Archduke Ludwig; and an **art gallery** displaying paintings by Joan Miró, Max Ernst and Antoni Saura as well as Mallorcan landscapes.

The adjoining 16th-century palace, the **Palau del Rei Sanxo** (hours as for La Cartuja, closes half an hour later; combined ticket), was constructed on the site of one Jaume II built for his son, Sanxo, and is entered through a tranquil, plant-filled courtyard. Piano recitals of Chopin's music are held throughout the day and Festival Chopin takes place here every August.

⊙ CATALINA TOMÁS

Santa Catalina is Mallorca's very own saint. She was born in Valldemossa in 1531 in a house at Carrer Rectoría 5, behind the church, which is now a shrine. In a quiet corner of Carrer de la Beatà, where caged birds sing, there is another smaller shrine with a fountain and ferns. Almost every house has a tiled picture outside, depicting scenes from the saint's life and asking her blessing: 'Santa Catalina Tomás Pregau Per Nosaltres'. She was a farmer's daughter, marked out as special when still a child, and taken to Palma by a sympathetic patron, where she worked as a servant in a wealthy household before entering the convent of Santa Magdalena and taking her vows.

AROUND THE TOWN

Outside the monastery is a cobbled *plaça* shaded with lime trees – *tilos* – which give the square its name. The streets around it, and those leading to the 13th-century church of Sant Bartomeu, dedicated to Santa Catalina, are bright with potted plants, and the steepest, most slippery parts are covered with strips of carpet to prevent people tripping up.

The main street in the lower town, where there are adequate car parks, is lined with cafés and restaurants and some interesting little shops, selling jewellery and clothes made of cool, natural fibres. One of the nicest bars (just back from the main street, on Carrer Blanquera) serves delicious *horchata*, fresh juice and good coffee and hot chocolate, along with *cocas de patata*, the sugar-dusted, potato-shaped buns, tasting not unlike *ensaimadas*, that are a local speciality.

On the edge of town, at Avda Palma 6, is the **Centre Cultural Costa Nord** (daily 9am–5pm), founded by Michael Douglas, who has had a home nearby for many years, and who narrates the commentary to a virtual reality tour of the region. There is also an exhibition here about Archduke Ferdinand (see Son Marroig) and a smart restaurant.

In the other direction, a few metres along the road towards Banyalbufar, a vertiginous road leads 6km (4 miles) down to the tiny **Port de Valldemossa** where there's a small gravel beach and crystal-clear water. On summer weekends, however, the narrow road and the limited parking area become uncomfortably busy.

SON MARROIG

The coastal Ma-10 continues north, with stunning sea views to the left, and groves of ancient, gnarled olive trees among huge boulders to the right. After about 6km (4 miles), a track signposted simply **Miramar** leads to the ruins of a monastery founded by Ramon Lull. Only part of the cloister remains, but there is also a chapel and a museum with artefacts collected by Archduke Ludwig. A short way further on, a sign points to **Son Marroig** ❿ (www.sonmarroig.com; Mon–Sat Apr–Sept 9.30am–7pm, Oct–Mar 10am–6pm), a manor house that belonged to the Austrian Archduke Ludwig Salvator of Habsburg-Lorraine and Bourbon, who had a life-long love affair with the Balearics and their people. Born in Florence in 1847, he renounced courtly life in Vienna and spent years travelling the world on scientific explorations, returning often to the estate he bought in 1870 on this beautiful stretch of coast. Several rooms can be visited, filled with paintings, photos and ceramics. In the gardens, there's a wonderful view from a cliff-edge white temple of Carrara marble.

Hundreds of metres below the house is **Na Foradada**, a rocky promontory, pierced by a remarkable 18m (60ft)-wide

The Teix massif forms a dramatic backdrop to pretty little Deià

natural window. If you visit the house, ask for permission to make the half-hour walk down to the sea and the landing stage where the Archduke used to anchor the *Nixe*. The restaurant near the car park is a wonderful place from which to watch the sunset. (For details of concerts at Son Marroig during the Deià International Music Festival, see page 94.)

DEIÀ

Set on the slopes of the 1,064m (3,491ft) Teix massif, **Deià** ⑪ is a delight, a pretty town of honey-coloured stone that has attracted artists, writers and assorted expatriates ever since the Archduke Ludwig first came here. He was followed by the Catalan poet and painter Santiago Rusinyol at the turn of the 20th century, and later by writer Anaïs Nin (1903–77) and the American archaeologist William Waldren. But it is Robert Graves, the poet and author of *I, Claudius* and the autobiographical *Goodbye to All That*, who came here with American writer Laura Riding in 1929, who is most closely associated with the place. Graves loved Deià and fiercely defended the northwest coast against commercial exploitation. It was largely due to his efforts that the area was designated a protected zone. His home, **Ca N'Alluny** (tel: 971 636 185; www.lacasaderobertgraves.com; Apr–Oct Mon–Fri 10am–5pm, Sat 10am–3pm, Nov and Feb–Mar Mon–Fri 9am–4pm, Sat until 2pm, Dec–Jan Mon–Fri 10.30pm–1.30pm) on the Carretera Deià–Sóller, has been restored and opened as a museum. The house and garden are delightful, and retain much of their original character as well as exhibiting the writer's effects.

You must leave your car on the main street, which is lined with restaurants, galleries and shops selling attractive summer clothes. Narrow, winding streets lead to the top of the village and the little church of **Sant Joan Bautista**. Beside it is a small

Cala de Deià

cemetery overlooking the Mediterranean; a simple cement slab bears the inscription 'Robert Graves, Poeta, 1895–1985'.

Deià is extremely popular, and many chic, well-heeled people have holiday homes here. Besides a luxury hotel, Belmond La Residencia (www.belmond.com), there are several less expensive alternatives (see page 137), and the best selection of restaurants on the coast (see page 109).

CALA DE DEIÀ

Just past the village, a twisting 2km (1 mile) drive takes you down to **Cala de Deià**, a tiny cove with a rocky beach, where ramps emerge from boathouses set into the cliffs. The water is clear, buoyant and safe and there are a couple of reasonable beach cafés. Don't imagine you've found a secluded beach, though. Regular visitors know it well and it can get very busy at weekends. You can walk to the beach, either by following

Sóller's Orange Tram

steps near the vehicle access road, or by walking down steep Carrer Bauza at the Valldemossa end of the village, following the course of a stream past pretty gardens until the village peters out and the path continues through groves of lemons and olives; it takes about 35 minutes in all.

SÓLLER AND ITS PORT

From Deià, the coast road, lined with groves of oranges, lemons and almonds as well as olives, descends into the broad valley of Sóller. The scenery is lovely and the town of **Sóller** ⓬ itself is a little gem, a busy, prosperous place that claims, like several others, to have been the birthplace of Columbus. It is full of well-preserved 18th- and 19th-century mansions, and the main square, **Plaça Sa Constitució**, with numerous cafés, is a good place to sit and absorb the town's character. Like the main street, the Gran Via, it has *Moderniste* (Catalan Art Nouveau) flourishes, including the church of **Sant Bartomeu**, and the former Banco Central Hispano (now Banco Santander) on the opposite corner, whose exteriors were designed by a pupil of Antoni Gaudí. About five minutes' walk to the east is **Can Prunera** (Carrer de sa Lluna 86; http://canprunera.com; daily 10.30am–6.30pm, Nov–Feb Tue–Sun 10.30am–6pm), a Moderniste house which is now a museum dedicated to the movement.

The station at the top of the town is another splendid *Moderniste* building. You can make an old-fashioned journey on a little wooden train that has been running from here to Palma and back on a narrow-gauge railway since 1912 (Tren de Sóller; journey time about an hour).

The station has another attraction, too: the **Sala Miró y Sala Picasso** (daily 10.30am–6.30pm; free), hung with drawings and lithographs by Miró and displays of some 50 ceramic pieces by Picasso.

Outside the station you can get information on hiking *(senderisme)* from the tourist office (tel: 971 638 458 or 971 638 008), housed in an old train carriage. Here, too, you can catch the **Orange Tram** that rattles on a scenic, 20-minute journey to **Port de Sóller** (www.trendesoller.com; departs every hour 8am–8.30pm; tickets sold on board), stopping en route where requested. This is a good old-fashioned little resort, with a fine harbour, and it has gained a few smart restaurants and bars in recent years. You can hire kayaks, take sailing or windsurfing lessons, take boat trips around the bay or further afield to Sa Calobra and Na Foradada.

TWO GARDENS

Just outside town, on the ring road, is the **Museu Balear de Ciències Naturales i Jardí Botànic** (www.museuencienciesnaturals.org; Mar–Oct Tue–Sat 10am–6pm, Nov–Feb Tue–Sat 10am–2pm) with a collection of aromatic

Tipico De Sóller

Sóller is a good place to try freshly squeezed orange juice *(zumo de naranja)*, as the orange groves around the town are reputed to produce the very best juice oranges. You could also sample the local orange liqueur, called Angel d'Or, which is used to flavour some of the cakes found on menus and in Sóller's many tempting cake shops.

herbs and plants from all over the Balearic Islands, fossils, a vegetable garden and a 'peace garden'.

The road from Sóller to Palma, with numerous hairpin bends and the 496m (1,627ft) **Coll de Sóller** pass to negotiate, was believed to be so daunting that it impeded the development of the area. Despite the protests of some environmentalists, a tunnel was constructed under the mountains, reducing travel time to Palma to about half an hour (the toll was eliminated in 2017 leading to a significant increase in traffic).

At the southern exit from the tunnel (on the left) are the **Jardins d'Alfàbia** ⑬ (www.jardinesdealfabia.com; Apr–Oct daily 9.30am–6.30pm, Nov–Mar Mon–Fri 9.30am–5.30pm, Sat 9.30am–1pm), a baronial mansion with wonderful gardens, that was once the country estate of a Moorish vizier of Palma. The cisterns, fountains and irrigation channels are a bit neglected, but the flowing water and shaded walks, with turkeys pecking under fig trees, and birds singing among exotic plants, are appealing. The house is full of treasures: look out for the huge, 14th-century oak chair in the print room, regarded as the most important antique in Mallorca. It's easy to see why this is such a popular wedding destination.

FROM BUNYOLA TO CASTLE D'ALARÓ

A few kilometres past the gardens a left-hand turn points to **Bunyola**, a peaceful little place that produces excellent olive oil and a bright green herbal liqueur called Palo Tunel. The village church and the town hall both stand on the main square, Sa Plaça, which is shaded by leafy plane trees. It's a lovely drive from here to the tiny village of **Orient**, which has a hotel (plus a few in the nearby area) and several restaurants and is a favourite base for hikers. The **Castell d'Alaró** ⑭ (www.castellalaro.cat), a ruined fortress built by Jaume I, crowns a massive crag 822m (2,700ft) high.

Fornalutx

You can walk up from Orient if you have lots of energy, strong shoes and a supply of drinking water, or drive most of the way to the summit up narrow, tortuous lanes, starting a little north of nearby **Alaró**. The tracks get progressively rougher, however, and the final stretch is only suitable for four-wheel-drive vehicles. Park before this section begins, at the restaurant Es Verger, and look for a sign saying 'Castell a Peu' (To the castle on foot). That leaves a 30- to 40-minute climb to do, not advisable in the heat of summer. The views from the top are spectacular. There is a small restaurant and simple accommodation, which must be booked in advance (tel: 971 940 503 or email reserves@castellalaro.cat; open year round).

THE HEART OF THE TRAMUNTANA

If you go in the opposite direction from Sóller, towards Pollença, the magnificent views continue as the road cuts through the heart of the Serra de Tramuntana and over the

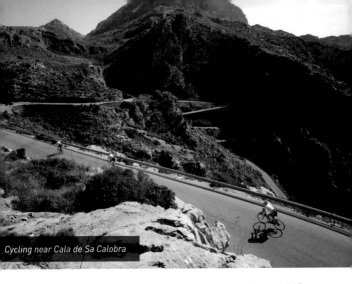

Cycling near Cala de Sa Calobra

pass of **Puig Major**, Mallorca's highest mountain at 1,445m (4,741ft). The range became a World Heritage Site in 2011.

Fornalutx ⑮ is an exquisite little town of warm stone buildings that has been designated a national monument – which naturally means that it draws in a lot of visitors, but also means building regulations are stringent. Set against the backdrop of the Tramuntana range, its steep cobbled streets are lined with cacti and palm trees. A high number of the well-restored medieval properties belong to foreigners, attracted by the region's beauty. The town is set among ancient terraces of citrus fruits and gnarled olive trees, marked out with dry-stone walls. Paths run through them to pretty little **Biniaraix**, which is also only a half-hour walk down narrow lanes, signposted from the centre of Sóller.

A short distance past Fornalutx on the Ma-10, the **Mirador de Ses Barques** has a restaurant where you can stop for a drink while enjoying spectacular views of Port de Sóller and the coast. The route then winds past the reservoirs of Panta de Cúber and Panta de Gorg-Blau, connected by a narrow canal. Near the latter, a little road leads down to the coast. Its name, **Sa Calobra ⑯** (The Snake), is an apt one for the 12km (8 miles) of hairpin bends that loop down to sea level. The views are stunning and the road is an adventure in itself, but try to come early in the morning to avoid the streams of tourist coaches.

Park where you can when the road reaches sea level and walk a short distance towards the deep gorge of **Torrent de Pareis**. Tunnels burrow through the rock to the riverbed where the gorge widens into a huge natural theatre. Be extra careful if it has rained, even only a little, as the rocks get very slippery. The idyllic little bay, **Cala de Sa Calobra**, has a couple of restaurants and bars and a pebbly beach, but they get crowded in summer.

MONESTIR DE LLUC

Around 10km (6 miles) further along the road to Pollença is the major pilgrimage site in Mallorca, the **Monestir de Lluc ⑰** (tel: 971 871 525; www.lluc.net; daily 10am–6.30pm, free; museum Sun–Fri 10am–2pm). Located in a valley near Puig des Castellot, the massive building mainly dates from the 18th century, but pilgrims have been coming here since the 13th century to pray to a dark-stone statue of the Madonna and Child, La Moreneta. According to legend, it was discovered by an Arab boy called Lluc, whose family had converted to Christianity. He took the statue to the church of Sant Pere in the tiny village of Escorça nearby, but it kept returning to the place where he had found it, so it was finally allowed to stay and a chapel was built to house it.

People still come to venerate La Moreneta, but many also come to have lunch and admire the views, as the monastery has a res-taurant, bar and barbecue area. It also offers inexpensive accom-modation; the rooms are pretty basic, but staying here allows you

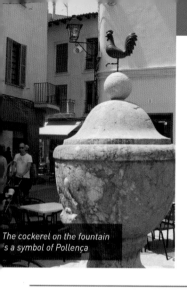

The cockerel on the fountain is a symbol of Pollença

to appreciate the peace of the monastery once the tour groups have gone home. If you attend Mass in the church during the school year you will have the pleasure of hearing the Lluc boys' and girls' choir, **Els Blavets** (Blue Ones), named after the colour of their cassocks. They also sing in the evenings, on Sundays and at special services.

THE NORTH AND NORTHEAST

The north is a region of great variety. It encompasses the rugged Cap de Formentor, the sandy coves of Sant Vicenç, two attractive towns – Pollença and Alcúdia – the resort of Port de Pollença and the huge, curved Badia d'Alcúdia, lined with resorts and facilities. Parallel to the bay is a complete contrast in the wetlands of the Parc Natural de S'Albufera.

From Palma, it is a fast drive up the Ma-13 motorway to the Ma-2200 turning to Pollença. If continuing the previous route, the road from Lluc curves through holm oak forests before descending to the Vall de Son Marc and Pollença.

POLLENÇA

Pollença ⑱ has a long history. The Romans established a settlement here after they moved inland from Pollentia (modern-day Alcúdia; see page 66), and the stone bridge to the north of the town centre is believed to have been built by them, although the actual origin of the bridge is still up for some debate. The Catalan community was founded in 1236 after the Moors were expelled. Present-day Pollença was first shown on a map in 1789; it was a prosperous town, the property of the Order of the Knights of St John until 1802, and able to support the numerous impressive churches still standing.

Pollença is a lively place, especially during summer evenings, when it is full with visitors; the comings and goings in the **Plaça Major** provide free entertainment for people sipping cool drinks outside one of several cafés and restaurants. The plaça also comes into its own on Sunday morning (8am–1.30pm), when local people shop for fresh produce in the market, then drink coffee outside the Café Espanyol (also called Ca'n Moixet), after attending Mass in the parochial church, **La Mare de Déu des Àngels**.

⊙ PUIG DE SANTA MARIA

Just outside Pollença on the Palma road is a path up to the **Santuari del Puig**, the ruined convent on 330m-high (1,083ft) **Puig de Santa Maria**. The first half of the 4km (2-mile) trail can be done by car, the latter part on foot. The dry-stone walls *(margers)* along the last section are a good demonstration of an ancient skill that is now dying out. The views from the top, stretching as far as the Serra de Tramuntana, Cap de Formentor, the plain of Sa Pobla and the bays of Alcúdia and Pollença, are superb. The 14th century Gothic convent began as a plea for protection against the Black Death but quickly became one of the most sacred buildings on the island. Accommodation is available and there is a bar and a restaurant (prior notice needed for accommodation, tel: 971 184 132).

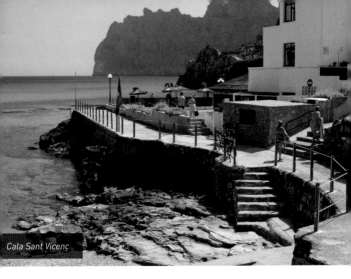
Cala Sant Vicenç

The Carrer de Monte-Sion, leading off the square towards the Jesuit church of the same name, has some great little shops and a number of restaurants. Good ceramics can be found in Ceràmiques Monti-Sion which has a display of old decorated tiles – unfortunately not for sale. Nearby is little Plazuela de la Almoina; the fountain has a cockerel on top, the symbol of the town. In Carrer Roca the **Fundació i Casa Museu Dionís Bennassar** (www.museudionisbennassar.com; Tue–Fri 10am–3pm, Sat–Sun 10am–2pm) displays the work and personal possessions of this local artist (1904–67) in his family home.

From the parish church in the plaça (or from the Ajuntament, off to the left), the **Via Crucis** (Way of the Cross), a flight of 365 steps lined with cypress trees, leads to **El Calvari**. This little chapel has been given a rhyming name – **La Mare de Déu del Peu de la Creu** (Mother of God at the Foot of the Cross) – after a 14th-century sculpture inside showing Mary at the feet of

Christ. At the bottom of the steps is the **Museu Martí Vicenç** (www.martivicens.org), which exhibits the works of the local artist, sculptor and textile designer.

Back in town, the deconsecrated Dominican convent and church of **Sant Domingo** (summer Mon–Fri 9am–4pm, Sun 10am–1pm, winter Mon–Fri 8am–3pm; free) is now devoted to culture rather than worship. Exhibitions of installation art are staged in the nave of the great 17th-century church in summer, and the cloisters are the venue for a classical music festival in July or August (see page 94), when an international line up of orchestras and soloists performs. Pollença's **Museu Municipal** (winter Tue–Sun 11am–1pm, summer Tue–Sat 10am–1pm, 5.30–8.30pm) is also housed inside the monastery in a large, light space. Somewhat eclectic, it includes changing exhibitions of contemporary paintings and sculpture, a permanent collection of Gothic art, some early 20th-century paintings and a few archaeological finds.

Outside the convent, the **Jardins Joan March Severa**, built around a watchtower, have an interesting collection of Balearic plants. The garden is always open but the watchtower is not accessible. Carrer Roser Vell leads off to the left; at its far end you will see the plain facade of the little 14th-century oratory of **Roser Vell**.

CALA SANT VICENÇ AND PORT DE POLLENÇA

About 3km (2 miles) along the Ma-2200 from Pollença to its port is the turning to **Cala Sant Vicenç ⑲**, a glossy resort built around three gorgeous sandy coves with brilliant blue water, excellent for swimming and snorkelling – although strong winds can get up quite quickly.

A couple more kilometres along the main road brings you to **Port de Pollença**. Set on the wide curve of a bay, with the marina in the centre, it has been popular with English visitors for many years and retains a distinctive atmosphere. However, it is a resort with a split personality. To the north of the marina the promenade has a plethora of restaurants, some with tables set on the beach, and a couple of stylish hotels. These give way to old, one-storey houses and wooden jetties, where the branches of trees almost reach the water.

To the south of the marina, however, the palm-shaded promenade that parallels the lovely, long sweep of sandy beach is lined wall-to-wall with cheap and cheerful tripper shops and fast-food joints. The narrow streets behind the promenade are nicer. There's a lot to do, however: sailing and scuba lessons are on offer, and there are boat trips to Formentor and Cala Sant Vicenç.

CAP DE FORMENTOR

Continuing round the bay to the southeast, towards Alcúdia, the commercial zone ends abruptly and the beach becomes a narrow strip, popular with windsurfers, with an expanse of lonely wetlands on the other side.

Hermen Camarasa

On the promenade north of the marina you may notice a memorial bust of Hermen Anglada Camarasa (1872–1959), the Catalan *Moderniste* painter after whom this stretch is named. He lived and worked in Pollença for many years. A collection of his work can be seen in the CaixaForum in the old Gran Hotel in Palma (see page 35).

But before heading in this direction, make a trip to the island's northernmost point, **Cap de Formentor** ⑳, the narrow headland on the north side of the Badia de Pollença. With sheer cliffs and idyllic sandy beaches, the rocky peninsula, surrounded by clear turquoise waters, is simply spectacular. The best place to appreciate the extraordinary landscape is the **Mirador des Colomer**, about 5km (3 miles) from Port

Cap de Formentor

de Pollença, where there is a specially designed walkway. Some tour buses don't go any further than this, which is a blessing for motorists, as the twisting road is a challenging one, demanding much concentration, and can get swamped with traffic in summer.

The pretty, pine-shaded beach (signposted Platja de Formentor on the right-hand side), is a favourite spot for a picnic and offers splendid views across the bay – similar to those you would get from the exclusive Formentor, a Royal Hideaway Hotel (www.barcelo.com). The hotel was built in 1928 by an Argentinian architect, Adam Diehl, and quickly became popular with a fashionable set, which included the Duke of Windsor and Mrs Simpson, Sir Winston Churchill and the Rainiers of Monaco, and is still the haunt of the rich and famous.

From the beach turn-off it's about another 12km (8 miles) to the lighthouse on the tip. Just before you enter the tunnel that leads through El Fumat, there's a great view of the sparkling

Alfresco dining in Alcúdia

waters of **Cala Figuera** far below, one of the most unspoilt beaches on the island.

ALCÚDIA

Retrace your steps now past Port de Pollença to the ancient, walled town of **Alcúdia** ㉑. There were Phoenician and Greek settlements here before the Romans founded their city in 123BC, and called it Pollentia (Power). They stayed for about five centuries before moving inland to present-day Pollença (see page 60). The Vandals sacked it, the Moors rebuilt it – Al Kudia (means 'on the hill') – and the conquering Spaniards fortified it in the 13th century. The massive walls and gates now standing are later imitations, but still impressive. Today, it's a nice, unpretentious little place, with some excellent Renaissance facades, good cafés and restaurants on the central **Plaça Constitució**, and a lively market held on Tuesdays and Sundays (8am–1.30pm), held just outside the walls.

The sturdy neo-Gothic church of **Sant Jaume**, which has a lovely rose window and gold altars, forms the southern bastion in the walls. Opposite the church, in a small, 14th-century building, is the **Museo Monogràfic de Pollentia** (summer Mon–Fri 9.30am–8.30pm, Sat–Sun 9.30am–2.30pm, winter Tue–Sat 10am–3pm). It has an extensive collection of Roman finds, including ceramics, glassware, tools and surgical instruments. You can pick up a free leaflet here describing points of interest in the Roman city. The remains of that city, the **Ciutat Romana del Pollentia** (hours as above), excavated in the 1950s by members of a dig organised by American archaeologist William Bryant, stand outside the walls (there's a large car park and a bus from Palma stops nearby). The area includes remnants of two buildings, and gives a good idea of the town's layout. The **Teatre Romà**, outside the city proper, on the road to the port, is impressive and the acoustics are great.

PORT D'ALCÚDIA AND THE BAY

Port d'Alcúdia has evolved from a small fishing harbour into an all-purpose port for commercial, naval and pleasure craft, and is one of the largest resorts on the north coast. Restaurants, cafés and discos have multiplied rapidly, as have high-rise hotels and apartment blocks, which now spread around the bay to form an almost unbroken ribbon of buildings 10km (6 miles) long.

To the east of the port, towards the Cap de Menorca, is the Fundació Yannick y Ben Jakober (www.fundacionjakober.org; Mon–Sat 10am–6pm, exhibition spaces are closed 1pm–2pm; free on Tuesdays 2pm–6pm, but access only to the Nins collection, Sculpture Park and Rose Garden), which displays portraits of children from the 16th to the 19th centuries. There is also a collection of contemporary art and a sculpture park.

The stretch of glorious white sand beaches along the **Badia d'Alcúdia** in summer is a mass of bodies soaking up the sun's rays or sheltering under colourful umbrellas. Although big, crowded and impersonal, the resort, which more or less merges into Can Picafort at the eastern end, does not have the seediness of some of the southern spots. Both remain low-key, if perhaps a bit soulless, and are good options for families with children or teenagers in need of entertainment.

As you drive along the main road, lined with supermarkets, shops and high-rise hotels, signs saying simply 'Platja' lead to the beach. The area around **Platja de Moro** is a bit quieter, but it is only just after sprawling **Can Picafort** that development ends.

PARC NATURAL DE S'ALBUFERA

About halfway between Port d'Alcúdia and Can Picafort, almost opposite the Hotel Parc Naturel (www.grupotel.com), is the entrance to the **Parc Natural de S'Albufera ㉒** (daily Apr–Sept 9am–6pm, Oct–Mar 9am–5pm; free). There's a car park a few metres further along. It seems remarkable to find this huge area of wetlands so close to major resorts and it can be a real haven for visitors as well as for birds, more than 200 species of which have been spotted here. A free permit must be picked up from the Reception Centre, about 1km (0.5 miles) from the entrance (9am–4pm). The reserve covers 800 hectares (2,000 acres), with walking and cycling tracks through it, and is criss-crossed by a network of canals constructed in the 19th century by a British company that began reclaiming marshland for agriculture, but ran out of money. The area became a protected zone in 1988, one of the first beneficiaries of the new environmental consciousness.

THE CENTRAL PLAIN

The centre of Mallorca is called **Es Pla** (The Plain). Lightly populated and not particularly geared towards visitors, there are lovely agricultural landscapes with ancient stone farmhouses (*fincas*), olive groves and unassuming old towns. It is known as 'the land of a thousand windmills' and while it's unlikely that anyone has counted, there certainly are a lot of them. They are a characteristic of the island, and many have been restored and put back into use, particularly around Sa Pobla.

Just one of Mallorca's 'thousand windmills'

This route starts at Pollença and visits several inland towns, with a detour to Randa, the 'monastery mountain', but narrow country roads run off in all directions and are worth exploring.

SA POBLA

The Ma-2200 runs about 12km (8 miles) through fertile farmland to **Sa Pobla**, an unexceptional but pleasant town with several fine old buildings around the main square and a church consecrated to Sant Antoni Abat. The Sunday morning food market is worth a visit and a jazz festival takes place in Sa Pobla throughout August.

From here you can continue down the main Ma-13 to **Inca**. It is not a particularly interesting town, but it is worth a visit for its *cellers* (see page 72) and for the factory shop selling Camper shoes.

BINISSALEM AND SINEU

Binissalem is about 8km (5 miles) further down the main road, in the heart of the wine-producing district. You will see vineyards stretching for miles around – particularly attractive in late summer, when grapes are nearly ready for picking. There's a wine festival here in September.

It's nicer, though, to take the rural (but good) road to **Sineu** ㉓, at the centre of the island, the pick of the inland towns. It has an elegant Gothic church, with some lovely reliefs by the Mannerist Gaspar Gener (1563–90), a baroque retable and some interesting modern stained glass. There are also some attractive baronial homes in the town, and a peaceful plaza with good restaurants. Its Wednesday-morning market (typically 8am–2pm), including the sale of animals, is the most authentic on the island. The building that once housed the **Centre d'Art S'Estació** remains on the outskirts of town, but its collection of contemporary art has been moved. In **Costitx**, 7km (4 miles) to the west of Sineu, the Astronomical Observatory of Mallorca stages astronomical shows (http://www.oamallorca.org; tel: 649 997 752; shows Fri–Sat at 8pm in summer and 7pm in winter; only by appointment) that are both entertaining and educational.

Festival of Pets

On 16 January, a popular festival in honour of Sant Antoni Abat is celebrated in Sa Pobla, with an enormous bonfire, music and the eating of *espinagades* (pastries filled with spiced vegetables and S'Albufera eel). The next day, the town's pets are led in a street procession and then blessed outside the church.

FROM PETRA TO THE SANCTUARIES

From Sineu it is about 11km (6 miles) to **Petra** ㉔. One reason people go to this sleepy little town is to visit the **Casa Museu Fray**

Juníper Serra (www.fundacioncasaserra.org; Tue–Sat 9.30am–1.30pm, pre-arranged visits only; tel: 664 366 722; book at www.spiritualmallorca.com). Petra is the birthplace of Fray Serra (1713–84); one of Mallorca's best-known sons, he was a Franciscan monk who founded numerous missions in California and was canonized Pope Francis in 2015. The museum, run by a dedicated Society of

Colourful shutters in Sineu

Friends, illustrates these and other New World missions; his house next door is more interesting, a modest place with cell-like rooms and a pretty garden. Wall tiles on the usually closed monastery of Sant Bernardino, opposite, depict the Californian missions; and signs lead to Es Celler (see page 72).

From Petra it is less than 5km (3 miles) on the Ma-3320 to the main Palma road (MA-15). The first town en route in the direction of Palma is Vilafranca de Bonany, known for the production of sweet little tomatoes, garlic, red peppers and melons. A little further along, a turning on the right takes you to **Els Calderers de Sant Joan** (www.elscalderers.com; daily Apr–Oct 10am–6pm, Nov–Mar 10am–5pm), an 18th-century manor house with a chapel, a granary and an extensive estate and farm. You can sample homemade products as part of a tour.

Still heading towards Palma, turn off at Algaida to visit **Puig de Randa**, the highest point on the plain at 543m (1,781ft), crowned by the **Santuari de Nostra Senyora de Cura** ㉕ (tel: 971 120 260; www.santuaridecura.com; museum and church hours summer 10am–1.30pm and 3pm–6pm, winter 10am–1.30pm and 3pm–5pm), which has accommodation and a bar-restaurant. The philosopher and mystic Ramón Llull (1235–1316) established the original sanctuary. On your way up you pass the Oratori de Gràcia and the hermitage of Sant Honorat. Randa is the centre of a little cluster of sanctuaries. Not far away, the **Ermita de la Pau** has a Romanesque chapel; and just above the village of Porreres you can drive the 4km (2.5 miles) up to the **Santuari de Monte-Sión**, which contains a 15th-century marble statue of the Verge de Monte-Sión.

To return to Palma, continue on the Ma-15 or get onto the motorway (MA-19) at Llucmajor. For the east coast, take the Ma-15 towards Manacor, then north to Artà.

⊘ CELLERS

Anyone interested in the true *cuina Mallorquina* – Mallorcan cooking – should visit a *celler*. These cool basement bodegas were originally wine shops and are still lined with huge oak barrels, but have now become restaurants, serving large helpings of island food. They exist all over the island, but there are some especially renowned ones in the inland towns. Inca has about half a dozen, of which Can Amer (www.celler-canamer.es) is the best known. In Sineu, the Cellar Ca'n Font on the main square is the place to go, while the best one in Petra is Es Celler (www.restaurantesceller.com) (see page 111 for details). They won't suit anyone who wants to eat outside in the sun, but their cavernous depths can be refreshing on a hot day.

THE EAST AND SOUTHEAST

The bays and beaches along the east coast have become slightly overdeveloped and overcrowded, but the resorts are nicer and far less excessive than those around the Bay of Palma, and some spots – harbours such as Port Colom and Cala Figuera – are delightful. There are also two fortified towns in the northeast corner – Artà and Capdepera

Cruising off Cala Mesquida

– and several amazing caves to visit, plus the Bronze Age sites of Ses Països (near Artà) and Capocorp Vell, near the south coast.

ARTÀ AND SES PAÏSSES

Artà ㉖ lies 12km (8 miles) inland, a fortified town that has retained a friendly, everyday atmosphere, and not become a mere showcase for its historic sites. It has a few good hotels with restaurants (see pages 112 and 142) and is a good place to stay if you want to escape the razzle-dazzle of the coast.

In a palazzo on the Plaça d'Espanya, the recently renovated **Museu Regional d'Artà** (www.museuarta.com; Tue–Sat 10am–2pm) stands next to the town hall and has a number of archaeological finds dating from the Phoenician, Greek and Roman periods, as well as a natural science collection.

The ancient church of the **Transfiguració del Senyor**, with a large rose window above the main portal, is one of Artà's major sites. Beyond, the Via Crucis (Way of the Cross), a broad flight of steps flanked by cypress trees and stone crosses, leads to the **Santuari de Sant Salvador d'Artà**. Construction started in the 13th century on the remains of a Moorish structure and today you can walk along the walls of this fortress, providing splendid views across the plain to the coast. You may be lucky and arrive while a recital is being given in the church – a wonderful experience.

The prehistoric settlement of **Ses Païsses ㉗** (Mon–Fri 10am–5pm, Sat 10am–2pm) is about 2km (1 mile) southeast of Artà on the Camí Corballa. A path leads from the shady car park through an impressive gateway in the Cyclopean wall surrounding the settlement. The ruins, set among holm oaks, include several square foundations, a *talayot* (tower) with a small chamber at its base, and an oval room called a *naveta*, with the remains of several pillars.

ew from Capdepera's castle

CAPDEPERA

Barely 8km (5 miles) east of Artà is the ochre-coloured town of **Capdepera**, its streets filled with flowers. Steps lead from the Plaça d'Espanya to the **Castell de Capdepera** (www.castellcapdepera. com; daily mid-Mar–mid-Oct 10am–10pm, mid-Oct–mid-Mar 9am–5pm). The largest castle in Mallorca, it originated in Roman times, was enlarged by the Moors enlarged it and strengthened further by the Christians. Below the defensive wall, from which there is a superb view, stands the 19th-century church of Sant Bartomeu.

From Capdepera a road runs through farmland, past the Canyamel Golf Club (www.canyamelgolf.com), where a new road layout promises urbanisation to come, then winds high above the **Platja Canyamel** development to the **Coves d'Artà** ❷⓭ (daily Apr–June and Oct 10am–6pm, July–Sept until 7pm, Nov–Mar until 5pm; guided tours in English last around 35–40 mins). Carved out of the sheer cliff face, the caves are less commercialised than the Coves del Drac (see page 76) and the limestone rock formations are quite awesome. In the summer, you can get a boat here from Cala Ratjada.

CALA RATJADA

It is only 3km (2 miles) from Capdepera to **Cala Ratjada** (also spelled Rajada), a busy resort built on a grid pattern. It was once the most important fishing harbour on the island, after Palma, but much of the port is now used for leisure and pleasure, as you can see from the boats moored here. There is plenty of accommodation, although much of it is pre-booked by German tour companies; and a rash of fast-food outlets and tourist-tat shops can detract from the atmosphere. However, much of the seafront is attractive, with restaurant tables set among pines and succulents. There is one sandy beach in the centre of town, where good waves attract surfboarders, but most people head to the beaches a little further north. The northernmost one is **Cala Mesquida**, with beautiful, protected dunes and excellent surfing waves.

The **Platja de Son Moll** to the south of the resort can be reached via the promenade. Still further south is **Sa Font de Sa Cala**, named after a freshwater spring that flows directly into the sea. Here, a lovely little beach has been completely overwhelmed by two huge hotel complexes.

On a hill above Cala Ratjada's harbour, the **Jardins Casa March** can only be visited by appointment with the tourist office (tel: 971 819 467; www.fundacionbmarch.es), but the impressive modern sculpture displayed there makes it worth the effort.

CALA MILLOR TO PORTO CRISTO

The next resort complex, the largest and loudest on the east coast, is **Cala Millor**, where three separate *calas* merge together along the sandy beach of Son Severa. The resort is still growing, and the neighbouring promontory of **Punta de N'Amer**, a 200-hectare (495-acre) nature reserve, is the only area that hasn't been developed.

The road south passes the Safari-Zoo (see page 96) before reaching **Porto Cristo**, an old-fashioned resort with a pleasant, local atmosphere. There is a huge yacht marina, an unremarkable beach and a couple of traditional hotels vying with modern buildings. It's popular with Mallorcan visitors at weekends, and the narrow streets can get clogged.

Up Up and Away

A unique way to see the island is from the air. Mallorca Balloons (Carrer Farallo 4, Cala Ratjada; tel: 971 596 969; www.mallorcaballoons.com) offer several different flights including trips over the Serra de Tramuntana, moonlight flights, breakfast flights and trips to see the almond blossom in bloom.

Most of the tour buses here are ferrying visitors to the **Coves del Drac** ㉙ (www.cuevasdeldrach.com; daily mid Mar–Oct 10am–5pm, Nov–mid Mar 10.45am–3.30pm), south of town. Seven daily tours in summer (four in winter) run through 2km (1 mile) of brightly lit chambers and spectacular formations, culminating with classical music recitals and boat trips on the 177m (581ft)-long subterranean lake named after Edouard-Alfred Martel, the French speleologist who explored the caves in 1896.

On the road to Manacor, the **Coves dels Hams** (www.cuevasdelshams.com; daily end of Mar–June 10am–5pm, July–29 Oct 10am–5pm, 30 Oct–15 Nov 10am–4.30pm, mid-Nov–Mar 10am–4pm) are competing for subterranean custom by offering a digital 'virtual adventure'.

Market day in Felanitx

FELANITX AND THE SANTUARI DE SANT SALVADOR

It's a pleasant drive south through agricultural land, with minor roads leading off to beaches. To the right, just before Porto Colom, is **Felanitx** – you will see watchtowers on the hill as you approach. This was the birthplace, in 1957, of the painter Miquel Barceló, and it is a good place to buy ceramics. There is a lively market on Sunday morning, and an impressive, partly 13th-century church, Sant Miquel.

En route to Felanitx, turn off to the **Santuari de Sant Salvador** ⑳, 509m (1,670ft) above sea level. The first sanctuary here was built in 1348; today's structure dates from 1734. On one side of the hill is a 14m (46ft) stone cross, and on the other the monument to Cristo Rei (Christ the King). The monastery church contains a fine alabaster retable showing scenes from *The Last Supper*. There are also a number of championship cyclists' jerseys, fading in glass cases along with notes of homage to the virgin. You can drive right up to the sanctuary. There are magnificent views, and accommodation in the Petit Hotel Hostatgería Sant Salvador (tel: 971 515 260; www.sant-salvadorhotel.com), with bright, pleasant rooms and a good restaurant.

PORTO COLOM TO CALA MONDRAGÓ

Reached on the Ma-4010 from Felanitx, **Porto Colom** is still a working fishing port, where you can watch the daily catch brought ashore. There is a strip of beach along the bay but the lack of a significant, sandy beach has ensured that Porto Colom remains a pleasant place, with a pine-shaded promenade and some pretty, pastel-coloured houses. Holiday apartments line the streets inland, but the only real commercial development is around the bay at Cala Marsal, south of the harbour.

Cala d'Or is only 7km (4 miles) further south, but you have to go inland then return to the coast. A resort of many years standing, it has evolved into a huge, stylish complex encompassing several different coves and beaches. The architecture is pretty homogeneous – low-rise, flat-roofed and snowy-white. The coves are pretty and the swimming is good, the harbour plays host to some elegant yachts, and there are all the tourist facilities and water sports you could want.

If you want to get away from it all, you must go a little further south to **Porto Petro**, an attractive harbour with a yacht club and some nice restaurants; then wend your way to **Cala Mondragó**, which is off the beaten track and practically undeveloped in comparison with most of the coast. It should stay that way, because the two pleasant little sandy beaches are part of the 785-hectare (1,940-acre) **Parc Natural Mondragó** (information centre in the car park; daily 9am–4pm; free), which also encompasses farmland and wetlands. There are walking tracks through the park and plentiful opportunities to birdwatch and look for the wild orchids growing beneath the trees. A few hotels and beach restaurants are here but it's all very low key.

Cala Mondragó

SANTANYÍ AND CALA FIGUERA

Return to the main road and after 5km (3 miles) you'll come to **Santanyí** ❷, a mellow little town of honey-coloured sandstone with one gate, Sa Porta Murada, remaining from the fortified walls. The elongated Plaça Major has some friendly cafés, but is dominated by the huge church of **Sant Andreu Apostel**, which has a famous, ornate organ, and the adjoining **Església de Roser**, the original 14th-century parish church. There's an arty feel to Santanyí, with several exhibition venues, and a number of antiques and ceramics shops.

    Cala Figuera ❸ is delightful, a fishing port with neat green-and-white houses and a walkway alongside the boathouses right at the water's edge. A handful of leisure boats bob in the waters, but they do not outnumber or outshine the working vessels. There are plenty of restaurants and some

Cala Figuera

accommodation but the tourist industry has not gotten out of hand.

JOURNEY'S END

Back to the main road again, and the first stop after Santanyí is **Botanicactus** ③④ (www. botanicactus.com; daily Apr–Aug 9am–7.30pm, Sept–Oct till 7pm, Nov–Feb 10.30am–4.30pm, Mar 9am–6.30pm). It one of the better botanical gardens in Europe, and contains 1,500 different plant species. It's not all cacti – there's an artificial lake surrounded by palms, and a stunning assortment of indigenous flowers.

Some 7km (4 miles) away is **Colònia de Sant Jordi**, one of Mallorca's earliest resorts. Its pleasant harbour is the starting point for trips to Cabrera, and you can walk around the dunes to the south of the bay. To the west of Sant Jordi the sandy stretch of **Platja Es Trenc** is now a protected area, so major development will not be permitted. Its less populated areas are popular with nudists.

The main road west from Santanyí, through a flat, agricultural landscape where many of the windmills have been renovated with brightly coloured sails, goes to **Campos** ③⑤, a friendly town with two huge, sandstone churches. The Església Parroquial Sant Julià contains a painting by Murillo (1617–82) but it is usually only open for mass.

The road then heads to **Llucmajor**, an ancient town with a few striking *Moderniste* buildings. If you want to go straight to Palma, the new stretch of motorway will take you almost the whole way. Otherwise, follow signs to **Capocorb Vell** ㊱ (www.talaiotscapocorbvell.com; Fri–Wed 10am–5pm), the best-known Bronze Age site in Mallorca. The foundations of 28 enormous buildings can be seen, and at the edge of the settlement are two massive *talayots* and three round towers.

You can drop down to **Cap Blanc** ㊲, where a lighthouse stands on a rocky promontory. From here, the road runs along a rather dull stretch of coast towards the **Platja de Palma. S'Arenal**, the largest resort, merges into **Les Meravelles** on a 7km (4-mile) strip of packed beaches, fast-food outlets, high-rise hotels, high-throttle discos, English pubs, Murphy's bars and German beer halls. Approaching the yacht harbour of **Ca'n Pastilla**, the road becomes pedestrianised and more pleasant – and then you are back in Palma.

⊙ CABRERA

Cabrera, an uninhabited island 17km (10 miles) south of Cap de Ses Salines, has been a nature reserve since 1991 (if not in a group you will need permission to visit; www. reservasparquesnacionales.es). It is only 7km (4 miles) by 5km (3 miles) in extent with a rocky coast and rugged limestone centre where a track leads 72m (236ft) up to the castle. There are two little bays, good for swimming and snorkelling. Bring your own supplies, or opt for lunch on a tour boat, because there is nowhere to buy food or water. During the Napoleonic Wars, Cabrera was used to house French prisoners, and it later quartered Spanish soldiers.

Sailing around the island

WHAT TO DO

SPORTS

Most outdoor activities in Mallorca revolve around the water and there is a great range of things to do, including sailing, wind-surfing, kitesurfing, paragliding, water-skiing, paddle boarding, snorkelling, fishing and, of course, swimming. However, walking, climbing and birdwatching are catching up in popularity, drawing thousands of visitors to the island, especially in spring and autumn, when the mild weather makes walking a pleasure, and numerous species of migrating birds delight birdwatchers. Mallorca is also a great place for cycling, horse riding and golf.

SAILING

The Balearics are a sailing paradise. The former king of Spain Juan Carlos can be spotted sailing around the coast every summer and British Olympic gold medallist sailor Sir Ben Ainslie is also partial to the area. The island has a wealth of safe harbours and some 32 marinas, and thousands of foreign visitors moor boats here year round.

You can **hire** various kinds of craft for an hour, a day or week at many beaches and hotels. The **Asociación Provincial de Empresarios de Actividades Marítimas de Baleares** is the biggest yacht charter company (tel: 971 727 986; www.apeam.com). The **Centro Náutico Port de Sóller**, Platja d'En Repic, Port de Sóller, tel: 609 354 132; www.nauticsoller.com, is recommended for boat or kayak hire and organises water-based excursions. The **Escuela Nacional de Vela Calanova**, Avinguda Joan Miró 327, Palma, tel: 971 402 512; www.port-calanova.com/es offers intensive beginners' courses; as does

Windsurfers have a wonderful time in Mallorca

Centro Náutico Port de Sóller. **Sail and Surf Pollença**, Passeig Saralegui, Port de Pollença, tel: 971 865 346, www.sailsurf.de is a prestigious club that offers instruction for beginners and more advanced sailors.

WINDSURFING AND WATER-SKIING

There are windsurfing schools, with equipment hire, at several of the larger resorts. **Sail and Surf Pollença** offers windsurf hire and tuition, as does **Water Sports Mallorca** (tel: 606 353 807; www.watersportsmallorca.com), which has a school in Alcúdia offering windsurfing, kitesurfing, surfing and catamaran classes. Also in Alcúdia is Spain's longest cable ski for wakeboarders (tel: 633 664 439; www.mallorcawakepark.com). On the east coast, windsurfing facilities are available at Cala Millor and Cala d'Or. Water-skiing equipment can be hired on many beaches, including Cala Millor, Can Picafort and Port d'Alcúdia.

SCUBA DIVING

Mallorca's crystal-clear waters, especially in the shallow coves on the south and east coasts, are ideal for diving. Scuba-diving equipment is available for hire if you have a qualification from your home country. The **Federación Balear de Actividades Subacuaticas**, Carrer de l'Uruguai, 07010 Palma, Illes Balears, tel: 971 708 785, www.fbdas.com, can give information and advice. The numerous scuba diving clubs include three in the southwestern corner: **Dragonera Dives (Aqua Marine Diving)**, Port d'Andratx, tel: 971 674 376, www.aqua-mallorca-diving.com; **Scuba Activa**, Sant Elm, tel: 971 239 102, www.scuba-activa.com; and **Big Blue Diving**, Palmanova, tel: 971 681 686, www.bigblue-diving.net, with numerous sites for people of all ability levels. In Pollença there's Scuba Mallorca, tel: 971 868 087, www.scu-bamallorca.com; and in the northeast, **Mero Diving**, Cala Ratjada, tel: 971 565 467, www.mero-diving.com, is well established.

BOAT TRIPS

There are trips available from various points along the west coast. In Port de Sóller, **Barcos Azules**, Muelle comercial, S/N Local 2-3, tel: 971 630 170, www.barcosazules.com runs a variety of trips around the rugged coast and tiny bays, including Sa Calobra. Boat trips operate from most ports, some using glass-bottomed boats.

WALKING AND CLIMBING

The Mallorcan landscape is perfect for dedicated hikers and more leisurely walkers. April and May, with a wild profusion of flowers, are the best months and September and October are good, too. In the hotter months, start early in the day or make use of the long evenings. Needless to say, correct footwear is essential and common sense will tell you that a supply of water, a wide-brimmed hat and sunscreen are wise precautions.

The **Serra de Tramuntana** makes for the most dramatic scenery, especially on the climb to Castell d'Alaró (see page 56) and between the Monasteri de Lluc and the coast. In the southeast corner, there are numerous walking trails through the pine groves, marshlands and dunes of the **Parc Natural de Mondragó** (information office open daily 9am–4pm, tel: 971 181 022; www.balearsnatura.com). These are on flatter terrain and more gentle than those in the northwest. There is even a Nordic walking park in Alcúdia. The tourist office in Sóller, tel: 971 638 008, produces a leaflet outlining walking excursions in the northwest of the island. There are walkers' maps available in bookshop La Biblioteca de Babel, Plaça Weyler 3, Palma, which also stocks

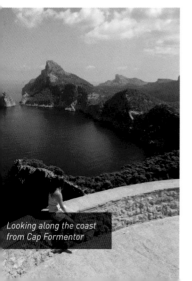

Looking along the coast from Cap Formentor

many excellent books on walking in Mallorca. In addition, the website www.camins-mallorca.info has lots of information.

There are also serious rocks in Mallorca for serious climbers. Contact the **Federació Balear de Muntanyisme**, www.fbmweb.com or **Grup Excursionista de Mallorca**, www.gemweb.org (website in Catalan only). Rocksport Mallorca (tel: 629 948 404; www.rocksportmallorca.com) offers courses for all levels.

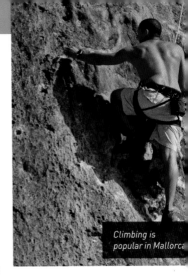

Climbing is popular in Mallorca

GOLF

There are over 20 18-hole golf courses in Mallorca, and all are challenging enough for even the best players. You can also hire equipment and take lessons. The beautifully landscaped **Arabella Golf** (tel: 971 783 000; www.arabellagolfmallorca.com) hosts a yearly 63 hole Golf Marathon while the course at **Golf Santa Ponça** (tel: 971 690 211; www.golf-santaponsa.com), is one of Europe's longest. On the east side of the island, **Canyamel**, (tel: 971 841 313; www.canyamelgolf.com), and **Capdepera** (tel: 971 818 500; www.golfcapdepera.com), are both popular. For further information, contact the **Federació Balear de Golf**, Cami Son Vida 38 - 1º, Palma, tel: 971 722 753; www.fbgolf.com.

BIRDWATCHING

Mallorca is one of the most rewarding birdwatching sites in Europe. The island's resident birds are enticing enough, but it's the visiting species that generate most excitement. Migrant birds stop off in spring – as many as 200 species have been spotted – and some stay for the summer. The most rewarding sites are the **Tramuntana** region, where rare black vultures and other birds of prey can be seen; the **Parc Natural de Mondragó** (tel: 971 181 022) for marine birds; and the **Parc Natural de S'Albufera** (tel: 971 892 250, www.balearsnatura.com), probably the best wetland site on any Mediterranean island, for the widest variety of all. Head to the birdwatching centre in La Gola (Carrer Temple Fielding; Mon–Sat 8am–1pm), Port de Pollença for further information. Also check the Mallorca Birdwatching website: www.mallorcabirdwatching.com.

HORSE RIDING

There are a number of small ranches and stables scattered all over the island, and some *agroturisme* properties offer treks or can arrange them for you. A few of the reputable riding schools are: **Ranxo Ses Roques** (Port d'Alcudia, tel: 971 892 809; www.ranxosesroques.com), **Rancho Jaume** (Porto Petro, tel: 629 627 063; www.rancho-jaume.eu) and **Hípica Formentor** (tel: 39 791 9232; http://hipicaformentor.com), which offers treks on well-cared-for rescue horses.

CYCLING

Bikes can be hired at most resorts. Check brakes and tyres and make sure a lock and puncture kit are included. Ask at the local tourist office for information on cycling routes. In Palma, bikes can be hired by the hour or day at Palma on bike, Av. Gabriel Roca 15, tel: 971 286 590, www.palmaonbike.com (they also organise bike tours, and hire rollerblades and kayaks), Bikehead (tel: 699 452 869; http://bikehead.cc). Always carry ID.

SPECTATOR SPORTS

Football is as popular in Mallorca as in other parts of Spain and there are dozens of clubs. In 2016, American businessman Robert Sarver purchased **RCD Mallorca** (aka Real Mallorca) and since then the team has worked its way back into the Segunda Division. They play at Son Moix stadium at Camí del Rei, Palma (www.rcdmallorca.es). Tickets are usually available on the day.

Bullfights *(corridas)* are still technically legal, but a new law passed in 2017 (following a previous attempt to ban them outright which was overturned by the Constitutional Court) now makes it illegal for bulls to perform for more than 10 minutes; the use of sharp implements; or have horses in the ring. This makes the sport nearly impossible to stage. There are still three bullrings in Mallorca.

Shopping in Pollença

Horse races are held weekly, all year round, at the **Hipòdrom de Son Pardo** near Palma. Betting is organised through a centralised tote system.

SHOPPING

Shopping in Mallorca is more expensive than it used to be, but you will still find some bargains, particularly if you are looking for leather goods or glass. For designer labels, however, **Carrer Verí**, in Palma's old town, has some smart boutiques, as well as several antique shops; and **Carrer Estanc**, off the **Passeig de Born**, has a number of chic clothing and interior design shops. **Avinguda Jaume III** is the capital's major shopping street, lined with leather and clothing shops as well as a huge branch of Spain's biggest department store, **El Corte Inglés**, which has a supermarket in the basement.

LEATHER

The Balearic Islands are justly famous for their leather industries. Excellent shoes, belts and bags and some of the finest leather and suede jackets come from the islands. The focus of the leather industry is Inca, where you can shop at the factory outlets or the local market, although the goods may not be any cheaper than you will find in Palma.

If you like shoes, then you'll love shopping in Mallorca. You can go to the factory shop of the quirky shoe company **Camper** (on the main road around Inca), whose highly individual shoes have become well known. Camper also has outlets in Palma, in Avinguda Jaume III and Carrer Sant Miquel. Less trendy, but extremely attractive and comfortable are *abarcas*, the slipper-like sandals made in Menorca that have been worn by peasants for centuries.

LINEN

Mallorca's embroidered table and bed linens are quite attractive, and the market in Llucmajor is a great place to find them. Other towns known for good-quality embroidery are Manacor, Pollença and Artà. In Palma, you will see a number of shops selling fine, hand-embroidered linen – and a lot of others selling machine-made versions.

Books

An extraordinary treasure trove of English books can be found at **Fine Books**, Carrer Morey 7, Palma, tel: 971 723 797: three floors of jumbled volumes, with everything from first editions to nearly new paperbacks, prints and old photos.

GLASSWARE, POTTERY AND PEARLS

High-quality **glassware** has been made on the island for centuries. The **Gordiola Museu del Vidre** (www.gordiola.com) factory and museum, outside Algaida on the Palma–Manacor road, is a good place to go. You can watch glass blowing and see some of the antique pieces on which many current products are based. They have a showroom in Palma, at Carrer Victoria 2.

Pottery is another traditional craft. There are two main types of cooking pots: *ollas* (round) and *greixeras* (flat and shallow). **Siurells** are small, clay figurines painted in red and green, based on Phoenician and Carthaginian originals.

Olive selection

Mallorcan cultured (artificial) **pearls**, Perlas Majorica, manufactured in Manacor, are exported in huge numbers. One of the best places to buy them is at the (well-signposted) **Pearl Factory** (www.pearls-factory.com) on the main road outside the town, where you get a tour of the factory and have the biggest choice. You can buy them all over the island, including Palma at Avinguda Jaume III 15, but while prices don't tend to vary between shops, it's worth noting that they can be pretty expensive.

FOOD AND DRINK

Mallorca is known for its herbal **liqueurs**, and the popular aperitif, **Palo**, is a novelty. One of the most popular brands is Tunel. Look for it in bright green bottles with the train logo, and decide if you want the sweet variety *(dulce)* or the dry *(amargo)*. Also worth trying is the orange liqueur, **Angel d'Or**, made in Sóller;

as is wine from Binissalem, as you are unlikely to find it outside the island. **Olive oil** from around Bunyola is an excellent buy, not cheap but fine quality. **Olives**, too, are worth taking home. For a selection of Mallorcan varieties, in all shapes, sizes and shades, acquire a plastic container and fill it up by selecting from the large tubs on market stalls. For specialised food-stuffs the most fascinating place is in the old-fashioned little **Colmado Santo Domingo** in Carrer Sant Domingo, near the city tourist office. You'll spot it immediately as it's festooned with hams, sausages and strings of peppers and garlic.

MARKETS

Weekly markets are held all over the island, where everything from fresh farm produce (including live chickens) to leather bags, household linen, pots and pans, sunglasses and sandals are for sale. They usually start fairly early in the morning and finish around 1pm. Particularly lively ones are held in Alcúdia on Tuesday and Sunday, in Pollença on Sunday and Sóller on Saturday. On Saturday morning in Palma the **Baratillo**, flea market, is worth a peek, even if you don't want to buy.

ENTERTAINMENT AND NIGHTLIFE

A monthly guide to events in Palma can be obtained from tourist offices. Otherwise there are listings in the *Ultima Hora* (http://ultimahora.es/mallorca) and *Diario de Mallorca* (www.diariodemallorca.es), both in Spanish. For English go to the comprehensive website www.culturalpalma.com.

Palma has a lively classical music scene. There are two excellent concert halls, the Sala Magna and the Sala Mozart, in **Auditorium de Palma**, Passeo Marítimo 18, tel: 971 735 328 for bookings, www.auditoriumpalma.com. The Ciutat de Palma

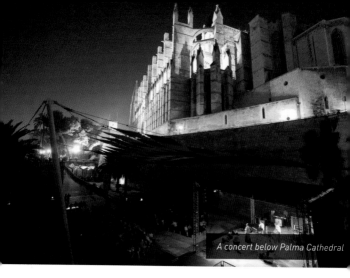

A concert below Palma Cathedral

Symphony Orchestra regularly performs here and there is a varied programme of orchestral music, ballet, jazz and opera. The **Teatre Principal**, Carrer del la Riera 2, tel: 971 219 700, www.teatreprincipal.com, stages opera, classical concerts and jazz; and the **Teatre Municipal**, Passeig de Mallorca 9, tel: 971 710 986, hosts dance as well as contemporary drama and films. In summer, concerts also take place in the music room of the **Palau March**, tel: 971 711 122, www.fundacionbmarch.es. Free outdoor concerts – jazz, rock and classical – are held in the beautiful setting of the **Parc de la Mar** below the city walls on some summer evenings. A bar serves drinks and snacks and there's a party atmosphere.

LATE NIGHT LINE-UP

The bars, clubs and discos in the big resorts thump with loud music all night long and would be hard to miss. Needless to say, they rise and fall in favour, and predicting next season's hottest spot would be unwise. They are mostly geared to the teen and early-twenties age groups and there is no shortage of leaflets and posters trying to tempt customers.

Otherwise, most of Mallorca's nightlife is to be found in Palma, where the best clubs are **Social** (https://wearesocial.club) on Avenida Gabriel Roca 33, a boutique nightclub with terrace overlooking the port; and **Tito's** on the Passeig Marítim (www.titosmallorca. com), popular with those who want to dance till dawn. Remember that the action doesn't really start until around midnight.

Outside the clubs, much of Palma's nightlife takes place in late-night bars, many of them in the Sa Llotja area, where most of the restaurants are. The kitsch **Abaco** (http://bar-abaco.es), Carrer Sant Joan (off Apuntadors), with its exotic decor, caged birds, operatic background music and expensive cocktails, is an

⊘ MUSIC FESTIVALS

Summer is the time for music festivals, most held in beautiful historic buildings. The best known one is the Deià International Music Festival (www.dimf.com). Most performances are in the stunning setting of Son Marroig (tel: 678 989 536). The Chopin Festival is held in the cloister of La Cartuja in Valldemossa (tel: 971 612 351, www.festivalchopin.com); and the Festival de Pollença (tel: 971 534 011; www.festivalpollenca.com) attracts international musicians to the lovely cloister of Sant Domingo. There is a summer music festival with performances in Palma's Castell de Bellver (tel: 971 735 065) and in the Jardins Fundació March in Cala Ratjada (www.fundacionbmarch.es). Sa Pobla hosts an international jazz festival in August (http://www. sapobla.cat) and Palma stages events in various venues as part of the Jazz Voyeur Festival (tel: 971 905 292).

experience. **Jazz Voyeur Club** (https://www.jazz-voyeurclub.com), Carrer Apuntadores 5, is a small, intimate place that offers a mixture of live jazz and blues from 8.30pm Tue–Sun; **Blues Bar**, Avda Miramar 28, plays, as you would expect, blues. **El Garito** (www.garitocafe.com), Dàrsena de Can Barbarà (near the Club de Mar) has a range of different club nights. For all the latest information on clubbing in Magaluf see www.feelsummer.com, while Mallorca Rocks has gigs by the coolest British bands from June to September.

Coves d'Arta

CHILDREN

Sandy beaches and calm, safe waters ensure that children can be happy on the beach for days at a time. But if that begins to pall, there are plenty of alternatives. The big resorts have a lot to offer in terms of entertainment such as water parks; they are quite expensive, but you can easily spend a whole day in them, which means you get your money's worth.

In S'Arenal, **Aqualand**, Palma–Arenal motorway, exit 13, tel: 971 440 000, www.aqualand.es, with its mega-water slides, claims to be the biggest aquatic park in Europe. **Western Park**, Carretera Cala Figuera–Sa Porrassa, Magaluf, tel: 971 131 203, www.westernpark.com, has adrenaline-pumping slides and high-diving exhibitions. All open daily (May–Oct) at 10am and there are special buses from the nearby resorts. In the north, **Hidropark** (www.hidroparkalcudia.com), Avinguda Tucán, Port d'Alcúdia, caters for younger children as well.

For older children and teenagers, there is **Magaluf Karting**, Carretera Cala Figuera–La Porrasa, tel: 971 131 734, www. kartingmagaluf.com, next to the Aquapark; and **Can Picafort Karting**, near Alcúdia, tel: 971 850 748, www.kartingcanpica-fort.com.

Safari-Zoo, Ctra Porto Cristo–Cala Millor, tel: 971 810 909/10, www.safari-zoo.com, on the east coast is usually a hit. The monkeys, antelopes, elephants, giraffes and rhinos can be observed from a mini-train, or from your own car. Fascinating for adults and children is the huge **Palma Aquarium**, Carrer Manuela de los Hereros i Sorà 21, tel: 902 702 902, www.pal-maaquarium.com. The **Acuario de Mallorca**, Gambí 7, Porto Cristo (next to the Coves del Drac), tel: 971 820 971, is smaller but also appeals to older children. The animals and the birds of prey at **La Reserva Puig de Galatzó** (http://lareservamal-lorca.com) are also popular. Katmandu Park, tel: 971 134 660; www.katmandupark.com, is a theme park in Magaluf mainly aimed at teens and adults, while its sister attraction in Palma Nova, **Golf Fantasia** (tel: 971 135 040; www.golffantasia.com), has crazy golf for all ages. Musical show **Pirates Adventure**, tel: 971 130 411; www.piratesadventure.com, also in Magaluf, is a spectacular evening out for all ages. Festival Park, near Marratxi, is a shopping outlet with lots of different boutiques, restaurants, a cinema, bowling and an indoor play area.

There are the **Coves del Drac** at Porto Cristo, the **Coves d'Artà** at Canyamel, and the **Coves dels Hams**, Carretera Porto Cristo–Manacor, which stage a digital 'virtual adventure'.

CALENDAR OF EVENTS

5–6 January: Three Kings (Reyes Magos) Procession in Palma.

16–17 January: Sant Antoni Abat festival in Palma, Artà, Sa Pobla and Manacor; a procession of animals to be blessed by their patron saint.

19–20 January: Sant Sebastià celebrated in Palma and Pollença, where the *cavallets* (small papier-mâché horses that the dancers strap round their hips) perform in a procession.

February: Carnival (Carnaval) celebrated in many towns and villages, with fancy dress parades and general revelry. This is a pre-Lent festival so dates vary depending on Easter.

March–April: Semana Santa (Holy Week) is celebrated in Palma and throughout the islands with solemn processions. In Pollença the Devallament (Lowering) sees a figure of Christ brought down from the Oratori on the hill.

8–10 May: Cristianos i Moros festival, also called Ses Valentes Dones, in Sóller re-enacts a battle in 1561 when local women fought against invading Turkish pirates.

13 June: Sant Antoni de Padua festival in Artà. Lively festivities involve *cavallets* and black demons that cavort around the streets.

15–16 July: Día del Verge del Carmen, the patron saint of fishermen and sailors, is celebrated in many ports with processions on the water. Palma, Port de Sóller and Cala Ratjada are the principal venues.

Late July: Sant Jaume in Alcúdia is a big religious and secular festival.

24 August: Sant Bartomeu is celebrated in Capdepera and Montuïri with horse races and devil dancers.

28 August: Sant Agustí fiesta in Felanitx, with *cavallets* (carousels) and *cabezudos* (big papier-mâché heads).

September – first Sunday: Processó de la Beatá in Santa Margalida.

Last Sunday in September or first in October: the Festa dies Butifarró in Sant Joan, with folk dancing and feasting on the famous Mallorcan black pudding *(butifarró)*.

31 December: Festa de Standa in Palma commemorating the Christian reconquest of the island under Jaume I in 1229, with a procession.

EATING OUT

Restaurants in Mallorca cover a wide spectrum, from the excellent to the mediocre, from the local to the international. You will find traditional, rural cooking – the hearty *cuina mallorquina* – as well as ubiquitous Spanish dishes like *paella* and *gazpacho* that are very popular although they have little to do with the island. There has also been a recent emphasis on Basque cooking, which is regarded as one of the best regional cuisines in Spain; and there are refined dishes with a French flair in the more expensive restaurants. Several top-notch chefs are working on the island and, while a meal in one of their restaurants is not cheap, it is considerably less expensive than it would be in one of the European capitals. At the other end of the market there are, of course, such staples as chicken and chips, pizza, bratwurst and sauerkraut for people staying in the popular resort towns and prefer to stick with what they know. Our list of recommended restaurants will help you make some informed choices (see page 107).

CUINA MALLORQUINA

Much of the best cooking derives from simple, country fare, cooked in olive oil and made from whatever fresh ingredients are in season. *Cuina mallorquina* reaches its height in *cellers* (see page 72) but can be found in many other places, too. A meal usually starts with a dish of multi-coloured, oddly shaped and quite delicious olives and a basket of rough-textured bread being brought to the table. There is sometimes a small charge for this, sometimes it is on the house.

Sopas mallorquinas – invariably referred to in this plural form – is a combination of vegetables, olives, garlic and sometimes pork. It is more like stew than soup, and makes

Restaurants in the Plaza Mayor, Pollença

a substantial first course. The *sopas* are usually served in an earthenware bowl, or *greixera de terra*, which in turn gives its name to a complete range of casseroles: *greixonera de peix* is a fish stew, and *greixonera d'alberginies* (or *berenjenas* in Castilian) is a wonderful aubergine concoction.

Another speciality is *tumbet*, a dish of peppers, aubergines, tomatoes and potatoes, coated in beaten egg and baked in the oven. This usually features as a first course, but can be very filling so should be followed by something fairly light. *Frit mallorquí* is a tasty mixture of strips of fried liver and kidney, peppers and leeks.

MEAT

Every rural family on the island once kept pigs, and many still do. Pork and its by-products are a mainstay, therefore, including *butifarró* (a spicy sausage, either white or dark), *sobrasada*, a bright red, pork-and-red-pepper-sausage with a consistency

Caldereta de langosta

rather like pâté, and *jamón serrano* or *jamón iberico*, a delicious cured ham, cut from a whole piece hanging from the ceiling.

Other popular dishes are *llomb amb col* (pork with cabbage and raisins); and *arròs brut* (rice with pork or chicken). *Lechona asada* (roast suckling pig) is really a Christmas dish but may sometimes be found on menus at other times.

You don't see a great many cows in Mallorca, so there's not a lot of beef in the restaurants, although some of the more expensive places serve delicious steaks. Chicken – *pollo* – is fairly common, though, and goat – *cabrito* – turns up on country menus, usually grilled, sometimes in a stew. Rabbit (*conejo*), is popular, sometimes served in a *greixonera* (stew), or *à la plancha* – grilled, and accompanied by *allioli*, a garlic mayonnaise; *conejo con caracoles*, rabbit with snails, is a favourite dish.

Snails (*caracoles*) are something of an acquired taste, but one that the islanders acquired long ago. At times they can be a free source of protein: after it has rained you'll see people out carrying string bags full of sand. They're looking for snails, which they clean by leaving them for several days in the sand, before cooking them and then eating them with *allioli*. Purists insist that true *allioli*, which is sometimes also served with the bread and olives that arrive at the start of a meal, should be made simply with oil and garlic, without the addition of eggs.

FISH

Really fresh fish and seafood are becoming something of a luxury on Mallorca. The seas have been over-fished and local fishermen, in any case, could not keep up with demand in summer. If you ask, waiters will usually tell you honestly that much of the fish they serve is imported, frozen, from Spain's Atlantic ports. *Salmonete* (red mullet) is caught locally, so are sardines *(sardinas)* and some of the *langostas*, spiny lobsters that are found on many menus. Locally caught *cap roig* – scorpion fish – is the choice Mallorcan fish; the cheeks are considered a great delicacy. *Caldereta de langosta* (*llagosta* in Mallorquí), a delicious lobster casserole, is a Menorquin dish, and an expensive one, that appears on some Mallorcan menus. *Zarzuela de mariscos* can be excellent – a thick stew of shellfish, tomatoes, garlic, wine and almonds.

☉ BREAD AND OIL

Mallorca, whose landscape is dotted with ancient, gnarled olive trees and once-functional windmills, is renowned for its bread and oil – so much so that Tomás Graves, the son of Robert, wrote an entire book about it, *Bread & Oil: Majorcan Culture's Last Stand*. The bread is dense and biscuit coloured, the oil thick and rich and green. So it is not surprising that *pa amb oli*, bread and oil (pronounced *pamboli*), is served everywhere. It is simply toasted bread rubbed with garlic, sprinkled with salt and lubricated with olive oil. As a refinement it may also be rubbed with fresh tomatoes *(pa amb tomàquet)* and served with cheese, local ham, *sobrasada* or even tuna. Cafés called *pambolierias* will give you your chosen ingredients on a large platter, plus a bottle of oil, and leave you to make yourself a tasty, filling and economical snack.

Fruit for Dessert

There is also fruit, of course: sweet melons, juicy oranges, peaches and nectarines, fresh figs and grapes, all the better because they are locally grown and have ripened in the field, not in transit.

Farmed trout *(trucha)*, sole *(lenguado)* and hake *(merluza)*, which are mostly imported into the islands frozen, also feature. Squid *(calamares)*, cuttlefish *(sepia)* and octopus *(pulpo)* cooked in a variety of ways, are also widely available. *Calamares en su tinta* is squid cooked in its own ink; *a la romana* means it is cut into rings and fried in batter – excellent when fresh and not over-battered. *Bacalao* is cod, salted and dried, and not to everyone's taste, but when well-prepared it can be good, especially in *esqueixada*, a salad of tomatoes, onions, beans and shredded salt cod.

SWEETS AND PUDDINGS

Home-made *crema catalana*, or its mass-produced cousin, known as *flan*, is as ubiquitous in the Balearics as the mainland, but there are also some wonderful sweet pastries and the almond and honey desserts that are a legacy of the Moorish occupation. Fig cake, a rich, dark brown confection with the consistency of Christmas pudding, is particularly popular in and around Sóller, a town also known for its *picos de* mazapán – little white pyramids of marzipan. Vegetarians should be aware that lard *(saim)* is an essential Mallorcan ingredient. It is a key element in the ensaïmada, the light, airy pastry that's rolled up like a turban, dusted with sugar, and eaten for breakfast, sometimes dipped in coffee.

DRINKS

Wine is usually drunk with meals, much of it imported from the Spanish mainland; Riojas and varieties from the Catalan

Penedès region feature prominently. But island wines are good, too, and some restaurants (especially the *cellers*) specialise in them. Most come from the region around Binissalem, which lies between Palma and Inca. Spanish beer is also quite popular. Fresh orange juice *(zumo de naranja)* is refreshing and delicious; and those who like the flavour of almonds should try *horchata de chufa*, a milky drink made from ground almonds that is served ice cold in summer. A local aperitif is *palo*, made from carobs and herbs and produced in Bunyola; and Angel d'Or, made in Sóller, is a local orange liqueur.

EATING HABITS

Local people eat late; lunch is between 1.30pm and 4pm, and any time before 9.30pm or 10pm is regarded as a bit early for dinner. However, restaurateurs, aware that northern European visitors like to eat earlier, have adapted their timetables accordingly. Remember that a restaurant that may look empty and unloved at 8pm may be packed and popular by 10pm. As breakfast is insubstantial – coffee and toast or a croissant – lunch is often the main meal. Islanders generally have three courses, but it's perfectly acceptable to share a first course, or to order *un sólo plato* – just a main course.

Binissalem produces a good range of wines

Many restaurants offer a *menú del día*, a daily set menu that is a real bargain; this is always available at lunchtime, and occasionally in the evening as well. For a fixed price, you get three courses – a starter, often soup or salad, a main dish and dessert, which is usually ice-cream, a piece of fruit or a *flan*, plus bread and a glass of wine, beer or bottled water. In restaurants where local people are eating, you will notice that many of them order the *menú*, an indication that it is not one specially designed for tourists.

Reservations are necessary only at the more expensive restaurants or places that are popular for Sunday lunch. Prices may or may not include VAT (IVA). They sometimes include service – look for *servicio incluido* on the bill. If not, it is customary to leave a 10 percent tip.

TAPAS

Tapas, the snacks that have become popular far beyond the borders of Spain, form a major part of eating out in Mallorca – at least in the bigger towns. They are still eaten as snacks, with drinks, which was their original role, but it is now common for a selection of these small dishes, or *raciones*, which are larger portions, to take the place of a main meal and this can be a relatively inexpensive way to eat. The advantage is that it allows you to be adventurous without making too many mistakes. The size of portions varies quite a lot, so be guided by a waiter as to how many dishes to order. As well as meatballs *(albóndigas)* and mushrooms *(champiñones)* you can try stuffed squid *(calamares rellenos)*, *pimientos de padrón* (small, green peppers grilled whole and sprinkled with sea salt), *spicy chorizo* or *espinacas à la catalana* (spinach cooked with garlic, anchovies, raisins and pine nuts). All are served with fresh bread to mop up the sauces and complement the strong flavours.

Can Joan de S'Aigo in Palma, Miró's favourite cafe

BARS AND CAFÉS

Bars and cafés are an important institution in Spanish life. In towns, some open at first light to cater for early-morning workers and most are open by 8.30am for breakfast. One of the great pleasures of the Mediterranean is sitting in a square in the morning with a *café con leche* (coffee with milk) or *café solo* (black coffee) and a croissant or *ensaimada* and watching a town come to life. In resorts, however, where many bars are open late at night and many tourists breakfast in their hotels, you may have more difficulty finding somewhere for an early coffee.

Wines and spirits are served at all hours. It is usually around 10 percent cheaper to have a drink at the bar rather than at a table. Sitting on a stool at the bar can make you feel like one of the locals, too, although it is not as relaxing as taking your place at an outside table and watching the world go by.

TO HELP YOU ORDER

Could we have a table? **¿Nos puede dar una mesa, por favor?**
Do you have a set menu? **¿Tiene un menú del día?**
I would like... **Quisiera...**
The bill, please **La cuenta, por favor**

DECIPHERING THE MENU

agua water
vino wine
leche milk
cerveza beer
pan bread
entremeses hors-d'oeuvre
ensalada salad
tortilla omelette
pescado fish
mariscos shellfish
langosta lobster
calamares squid
mejillones mussels
anchoas anchovies
atún tuna
bacalao dried cod
cangrejo crab
pulpitos baby octopus
trucha trout
carne meat
cerdo/lomo pork
ternera veal
cordero lamb
buey/res beef
pollo chicken

conejo rabbit
poco hecho rare
al punto medium
buen hecho well done
asado roast
a la plancha grilled
al ajillo in garlic
picante spicy
salsa sauce
cocido stew
jamón Serrano cured ham
chorizo spicy sausage
morcilla black pudding
bocadillo sandwich
arroz rice
verduras vegetables
champiñones mushrooms
judías beans
espinacas spinach
cebollas onions
lentejas lentils
queso cheese
postre dessert
helado ice cream
azúcar sugar

PLACES TO EAT

The following basic price guide (which is only approximate) is for a three-course à la carte meal for one, with a glass of house wine:

€€€€   over 70 euros
€€€   50–70 euros
€€   30–50 euros
€   below 30 euros

PALMA

Badal Burger €€ *Plaça del Comtat del Rosselló, 7, tel: 871 23 84 62*. It may not be fine dining but it is considered by some the burger place in the city. Gluten free options are available as well. Open Tue–Sat.

Es Baluard €€ *Plaça Santa Catalina 9, tel: 871 234 954*; www.restaurantesbaluard.com. Stylishly presented modern Mallorcan cuisine, including innovative dishes such as sticky rice and rabbit. Next to Es Baluard Museu d'Art Modern i Contemporani.

Bon Lloc € *Carrer Sant Feliu 7, tel: 971 718 617*; www.bonllocrestaurant.com. Palma's oldest and best vegetarian restaurant is situated on the ground floor of a 16th-century palace in the old town. It's open for lunch Mon–Sat and for dinner Tue–Sat, the menu changes daily and its mouthwatering dishes means the place is popular with carnivores too. Closed Sun.

Celler Sa Premsa € *Plaça Bisbe Berenguer de Palou 8, tel: 971 723 529*; www.cellersapremsa.com. This is a real institution, which has been operating for 60 years. They pair great ambience with a wide selection of classic (and filling) Mallorcan dishes. Mon–Sat 12pm–4pm and 7.30pm–11.30pm.

Forn de Sant Joan €€ *Carrer Sant Joan 4, tel: 971 728 422*; www.fornde-santjoan.com. Dining rooms on multiple floors in the heart of the old town restaurant area. À la carte Mediterranean dishes available, but it's essentially upmarket tapas – and very nice too. Also does a good gourmet menu for about €20 from 1pm–4pm.

Marc Fosh €€€ *Carrer de la Missió, 7, tel: 971 72 01 14; www.marc-fosh.com.* Enjoy premiere dining at a Michelin-starred restaurant. Amazing food and wine using local produce across the Balearic Islands, served amidst an enjoyable ambience. Also offers wine tasting. Daily lunch 1pm–3pm and dinner 7.30pm–9.30pm. Advance booking required.

Safrà 21 €€ *Carrer Illa de Corfú 21, Ciudad Jardin, tel: 971 263 670; www.safra21.com.* At lunchtime this restaurant specialises in serving traditional rice dishes whereas in the evening it becomes Mallorca's first 'Bistronomic' restaurant, focusing on top-quality cuisine at reasonable prices. Fri and Sat lunch and dinner, Mon–Thu and Sun lunch only.

Taberna de la Bóveda €€ *Passeig Sagrera 3, tel: 971 720 026; www.tabernadelaboveda.com.* There's usually a queue of tourists outside at 8pm each evening, waiting for the door to open, but this big, lively place is equally popular with locals, who come later. Excellent selection of tapas and mains. It's open for lunch too. Closed Sun.

13% € *Carrer Sant Feliu 13a, tel: 971 425 187; www.13porciento.com.* Just off Passeig des Born, this attractive wine bar serves excellent salads and plates of ham and cheese as well as fish and meat courses and an excellent variety of wine by the glass or bottle.

THE WESTERN CORNER

Andratx

Sa Societat De Ca Na Fornera €€ Av. Juan Carlos I, 19, *tel: 971 236 566.* Authentic Spanish cuisine at its best. Hospitable ambience, traditional meals and local wine. Mon, Wed–Sat 8am–10.30pm, Sun 8am–5pm, Tue closed.

Banyalbufar

Son Tomás €€ *Carrer Baronia 17, tel: 971 618 149*. A small bar-restaurant whose terrace commands outstanding views of the coast. Fish comes directly from the boats in the cove; paella and the *arroz negro* (black rice) are recommended. Closed Tue and mid-Dec–Jan.

THE WEST COAST

Deià

El Barrigon Xelini € *Archiduc Lluis Salvador 19, tel: 971 639 139*. Loud and lively, this popular place on the main road specialises in tapas and they come in all varieties. The stuffed squid is extremely good; the staff is friendly and casual; there's an outside terrace open in the summer months. Closed Mon and off-season.

Es Racó d'es Teix €€€€ *Carrer Sa Vinya Veia 6, tel: 971 639 501*; http://esracodesteix.es. Chef Josef Saueschell produces a modern menu in satisfying portions and has won a Michelin star. The *ballontine conejo* (medallions of rabbit) is delicious.

Sebastian €€€ *Carrer Felipe Bauza s/n, tel: 971 639 417*; www.restaurantesebastian.com.Lobster with asparagus ravioli and fig fritter with white chocolate mousse are two reasons to eat at this rustic-but-stylish restaurant where the Mediterranean cuisine often has a touch of the Far East. Open for dinner only and closed Wed.

Sóller

Bens d'Avall €€€ *Urb Costa Deià, Carretera Sóller-Deià, tel: 971 632 381*; www.bensdavall.com. About half way between Sóller and Deià, this gourmet restaurant with a lovely terrace overlooking the sea specialises in New Balearic Cuisine (nouvelle cuisine made with local produce). Open daily for both lunch and dinner.

Sa Cova €€ *Plaça Constitució 7, Sóller, tel: 971 633 222.* Pleasant restaurant on the main square. Serves good *conejo* (rabbit), which is popular in the area. The seafood stew – *cazuela* is worth the trip too.

QD €€ *Carrer Sant Ramón 1, Port de Sóller, tel: 971 632 804;* http://mesquidarestaurante.com. Lots of interesting salads and fish dishes, and a delicious tart made with the local Angel d'Or liqueur. Outside tables only, right by the harbour.

THE NORTH
Alcúdia

Bistró de Jardín €€ *Corner of Carrer Diana and Carrer Triton, Port d'Alcúdia, tel: 971 893 126;* www.bistrodeljardin.com. Value-for-money Mediterranean dishes from the sister restaurant of Michelin-starred Jardín (€€€€). Mar–Oct open daily 1pm–11pm, Nov–Feb Thu–Sat 1pm–4pm & 7pm–10pm, Sun 1pm–6pm.

Cala Sant Vicenç

Lavanda €€€ *Carrer Maressers 2, tel: 971 530 250;* www.hotelcala.com. An excellent restaurant in the Cala Sant Vicenç hotel (see page 139). The menu features refined Mediterranean cooking and there's a fine wine list. Set menu available. Open daily for dinner; closed Dec–Jan.

Pollença

Bar Nou Restaurante €€ *Carrer d'Antoni Maura, 13, Pollença, tel: 971 530 005.* This cosy restaurant was established in 1997. Run by the Torres family, this place is known for its paella and tapas selection. Delicious meals with flavours of homemade food. Closed on Wed.

La Font del Gall €€ *Carrer Montesió 4, Plaça Almoina, tel: 971 530 396.* Owned by a Scottish family, the Font del Gall, behind Plaça Major, serves a good range of dishes in a friendly atmosphere, indoors or out on a terrace.

Port de Pollença

Bellaverde Vegan & Vegetarian Restaurant €€ *Carrer de les Monges, 14, tel: 675 602 528.* The only vegetarian restaurant in this part of the island. Here you can enjoy your food and find shelter in the shadow of over 100-year-old fig trees. Tue–Sun 8.30am–11.30pm.

Stay €€ *Moll Nou s/n, tel: 971 864 013;* www.stayrestaurant.com. A stylish restaurant right in the centre of the port, that's been around for years. Fish is the first choice but there are meat dishes too, including lamb and pigeon ravioli. Open every day of the year.

THE CENTRAL PLAIN

Inca

Celler Ca'n Amer €€ *Carrer Pau 39, tel: 971 501 261;* www.celler-canamer.es. The best known of Inca's famous *cellers*, this family-run establishment has a long tradition of serving large portions of robust island food and a vast selection of wines. Open daily.

Petra

Es Celler €€ *Carrer de l'Hospital 46, tel: 971 561 056;* www.restaurant esceller.com. Huge and cavernous restaurant serving heaped plates of traditional food, including meat roasted in a wood oven.

Sineu

Celler de Ca'n Font €€ *Sa Plaça, Sineu, tel: 971 520 313;* www.canfont. com. Another one of the traditional cellers, Ca'n Font, in a hotel of the same name (see page 142), specialises in *sopas mallorquinas*, roast suckling pig and rice dishes.

THE EAST AND SOUTHEAST

Artà

Finca Es Serral € *Cami Cala Torta, tel: 971 835 336.* Enjoy Mallorcan and vegetarian cuisine in the rustic dining room or on the terrace of this attractive farm on the outskirts of town. Closed Mon and Nov–Mar.

Cala Figuera

Es Port € *Carrer Virgen del Carmen 88, tel: 971 165 140.* Eat inside or out, overlooking the bay. Spanish and Mallorcan specialities, fresh fish and good pizzas. One in a row of inviting-looking establishments. Closed on Tue.

Cala Millor

Tapas de sa caleta €€ *Passeig Marítim, 3, tel: 971 58 68 34;* http://sacaletacalamillor.com. Great service and even better food. As the name suggests, tapas is their specialty. However, their menu is varied enough to cater to all tastes. Daily 8am–11.30pm.

Porto Cristo

Vibes by Quince €€ Calle Bordils 51, *tel: 971 820 796;* https://restaurantevibes.com. You may be tempted to eat here just for the view as it's right on the water. However, their popularity is not just for the views as their fish dishes are especially good. Daily 11am–10.30pm.

A–Z TRAVEL TIPS

A SUMMARY OF PRACTICAL INFORMATION

A

ACCOMMODATION (See also Camping, and the list of
Recommended Hotels on page 134)

Hotel prices are not government-controlled, but rates are posted at reception desks and in rooms. Off-season, you can often get lower rates, although many hotels in resort areas close between November and March. In season, the majority of large resort hotels are block-booked by package tour operators. Breakfast is often but not always included in a room rate; check before booking. A value-added tax (IVA) of 10 percent and the Sustainable Tourism Tax ("tourist tax"; €4, €3, €2 or €1 per night, depending on the type of accommodation; under 16s go free) are added to the total; the 'tourist tax' is halved on the 9th day.

Accommodation ranges across a broad spectrum, although there are few pensions (guest houses). *Hostales* (modest hotels) are graded from one to three stars while *hoteles* (hotels) are rated from one to five stars. Recent years have seen more and more boutique hotels opening up as well as luxury resorts. Grades are more a reflection of facilities than quality: some two-star places can be superior to others with four. A new category – the *hotel d'interior* – has been introduced. These are small hotels (no more than eight rooms) which must be in traditional buildings, however minimalist their interior decoration may be.

Small hotels in rural settings and refurbished farmhouses and manor houses are called *finca* or *agroturisme* properties. They range from rustic to luxurious and many have minimum four- or seven-day stays; contact Rusticbooking (tel: 971 721 508, www.rusticbooking.com) for details. Rural Hotels Mallorca (tel: 0203 239 4983 [UK], www.ruralhotels-mallorca.com) caters for those looking for a more 'boutique' experience.

All-in package deals are the cheapest option and it can provide an economical base for exploring the island. If you want to rent a villa or apartment there are numerous agencies: www.majorcanvillas.com and www.mallorca.co.uk are reliable ones. Finally, there is the option of staying in a monastery or sanctuary, of which there are about eight (the *Where to*

Go section gives details of several) and the tourist office in Palma (see page 131) can provide a full list. These are fairly austere but extremely economical and popular with local people and outdoor enthusiasts.

> I would like a single/double room **Quisiera una habitación sencilla/doble**
> With/without bathroom and toilet/shower **con/sin baño/ducha**
> What's the rate per night? **¿Cuál es el precio por noche?**
> Is breakfast included? **¿Está incluído el desayuno?**

AIRPORT

Palma de Mallorca's massive **Son Sant Joan Airport** (PMI) is about 9km (5.5 miles) east of the city centre (tel: 913 211 000, 902 404 704; www.aena.es). Taxis and buses link the airport with Palma. Bus No. 1 leaves the airport every 15 minutes from 6am to 1.10am (until 2am in summer), running to Plaça d'Espanya, and to the port with stops en route (fare €5). There is a bus stop outside the car park, in front of the Arrivals Hall. Bus No.21 connects the airport with several hotels on Playa de Palma. Taxi is a lot faster than the bus, taking around 15–20 minutes. They line up outside Arrivals; the approximate fare is €25.

B

BICYCLE AND SCOOTER HIRE

A practical and enjoyable way to see the island is to hire a bicycle, and this can be done in most resorts – hotels and tourist offices have leaflets, and you'll be handed flyers in the street. Mopeds and scooters are also available, but you will need a special licence. Prices vary widely, so shop around. Remember that a helmet is compulsory when riding a motorcycle, whatever the engine size. Ask for a helmet and for a pump and puncture kit, in case you get stuck with a flat tyre many kilometres from your hotel, and always carry ID. In Palma, go to Palma by bike, Avinguda Gabriel Roca 15, tel: 971 286 590, www.palmaonbike. com. Pro Cycle Hire will deliver your bike direct to your resort hotel if arranged in advance; tel: 971 866 857 or check www.procyclehire.com.

BUDGETING FOR YOUR TRIP

Mallorca has become more expensive in recent years due to the fluctuating euro rate and the island increasingly becoming an upmarket destination. All prices below are approximate and given only as a guide.

Getting there. Air fares vary enormously. Flights from the UK with a budget airline can vary from around £70 return off-season to £190 or more in high season. Scheduled flights can be as low as £130 if you book well in advance, but anything up to £300 if you make a relatively late booking.

Accommodation. Hotels can be more expensive than on the Spanish mainland (for approximate prices in Recommended Hotels, see page 134). Rates for two sharing a double room during high season can range from as low as €55 in a *hostal* to as much as €400 at a top-of-the-range hotel. A comfortable, pleasant three-star hotel will cost about €100–€120. Rates drop considerably out of season.

Meals. The *menú del día*, a fixed price midday meal, is usually an excellent bargain, costing around €14 for a reasonably good three-course meal with one drink included. In a bar a continental breakfast (fresh orange juice, coffee and croissant) will cost around €6; a coffee €1.50–€3. The average price of a three-course à la carte meal, including house wine, will be about €35 per person. You can pay considerably less, but at top restaurants you may pay more than twice that much. The price of wine has increased: you will pay about €2.50–€3 for a glass of wine in a smartish bar.

Attractions. Most museums and galleries charge an entry fee of around €3–5. Entry to La Real Cartuja, Valldemossa costs €9.50; the Coves del Drach around €15. Water parks are more expensive, around €25 (children €18). A two-hour trip in a glass-bottomed boat costs around €15 (children half-price). You can usually find discounted and advance purchase tickets online.

Ferries. Inter-island ferries between Mallorca and Menorca are reasonable for foot passengers (about €50 return), but are more expensive if you take a car (between €100 and €300 for a vehicle and two passengers). The ferry from Mallorca to Ibiza is about the same price. Deals are often available, especially if you book well in advance.

C

CAMPING

Pitching a tent on beaches and parkland is illegal and you will be asked to move on. You may be able to camp on private land, but be sure to ask permission from the owner first or contact Rusticbooking, tel: 971 721 508; www.rusticbooking.com, for a list of farms that accept campers.

There are two official campsites, both in the north of the island. In Lluc, there is a campsite called Ca S'Amitger (Sa Font Coberta), tel: 971 51 70 70, which is only accessible by foot. S'Arenalet, tel: 971 17 76 52, is in the Levante natural park north of Artà, and another perfect place to get away from it all. Both are very basic in terms of facilities on offer, are only open for the summer season but are generally quite peaceful. Of course, for a truly peaceful experience it is best to go outside of the main holiday seasons.

CAR HIRE

The bus service is good, but if you want to travel a good deal around the island, hiring a car is advisable. Major international companies – Avis, Hertz, Budget, Europcar – and Spanish national companies have offices at the airport and in Palma as well as in the major resorts. Many have weekly specials which can work out as little as €20–25 per day. Rates are seasonal, and usually lower if organised in advance over the internet. Third-party insurance is included, but comprehensive insurance – *todo riesgo* – is usually extra. Be aware that insurance may not cover you for off-road driving. In addition to value-added tax (IVA) of

21 percent, an extra tax of €5 a day, controversially introduced to raise local revenue, is also payable.

Hirers must be at least 18 or 21 (minimum age varies depending on car type) and have (generally) held a licence for at least six months. Hire companies will accept your national driver's licence.

Avis: Avinguda Ingeniero Gabriel Roca 16, Palma, tel: 971 730 720, www.avis.es.

Europcar: Carrer Mar Menor, Las Maravillas, Platja de Palma, tel: 911 505 000, www.europcar.com.

Gold Car: Avinguda Ingeniero Gabriel Roca 29, Palma, tel: 918 344 064, www.goldcar.es

Hertz: Disseminat Aeropuerto son Sant Jo, Palma tel: 971 000 041, www.hertz.es.

Hiper: Camino de Son Garcias, Can Pastilla, Palma tel: 971 269 911, www.hiperrentacar.com.

> I'd like to rent a car. **Quisiera alquilar un coche.**
> for one day/week. **por un día/una semana.**
> Please include full insurance. **Haga el favor de incluir el seguro a todo riesgo.**

CLIMATE

The sea is pleasantly warm for swimming from June to October. July and August can be scorching and humidity may be high. Spring and autumn bring walkers and birdwatchers and those who enjoy sightseeing in cooler temperatures. Mallorca enjoys a mild winter, and many hotels stay open during the winter months. It can be chilly and wet at times but a wall of mountains along the northwest coast protects the rest of the island from the worst of the winter weather.

The average temperatures below apply to Palma, but do not vary greatly throughout the islands, except in the mountainous areas.

	J	F	M	A	M	J	J	A	S	O	N	D
°C	10	11	12	14	17	22	24	24	22	18	14	12
°F	50	51	54	58	63	71	76	76	72	65	57	53

CLOTHING

In summer you only need lightweight cotton clothes – although in June and September you may need a jacket or jumper for the evening. Remember also to take a sunhat and something with sleeves to cover your shoulders. During the rest of the year a light jacket and an umbrella will come in handy.

Although the tendency is towards casual dress, some restaurants, bars and clubs object to men wearing shorts and T-shirts and women being too skimpily dressed. Don't offend local sensibilities by wearing unsuitable clothes in city streets, museums or churches.

Walking shoes or good-quality trainers are advisable, of course, if you are planning any long treks.

CRIME AND SAFETY (See also Emergencies)

Spain's crime rate has caught up with that of other European countries and the Balearics have not been immune, although they remain one of the safest places in Europe. Be on your guard against purse-snatchers and pickpockets near Palma Cathedral and around the Plaça Major at night, and in markets and other crowded places. Take the same precautions as you would at home. In Palma, report thefts and break-ins to the Policía Nacional, elsewhere to the Guardia Civil. You need a police report for insurance purposes.

I want to report a theft. **Quiero denunciar un robo.**

D

DRIVING

Road conditions. There is a stretch of motorway around the city and the bay, west towards Andratx, ending at Peguera, and east to Llucmajor. Another motorway goes north via Inca and continues behind the town to Alcúdia. There is also a tunnel through the mountains (toll charged) from Sóller towards Palma. There's a good straight road running east–west across the island. Secondary roads are narrow but generally good; on the mountainous northwest coast there are numerous hairpin bends.

Rules and regulations. Drive on the right, overtake on the left, yield to vehicles coming from the right. Seat belts are compulsory. Children under 12 must travel in the rear. Speed limits are 120km/h (75mph) on motorways, 100km/h (60mph) on two-lane highways, 90km/h (56mph) on other main roads, 50km/h (32mph), or as marked, in densely populated areas.

Traffic police. Roads are patrolled (strictly) by the Guardia Civil de Tráfico, on motorcycles. Fines are payable on the spot. The permitted blood-alcohol level is low and penalties are stiff.

Fuel. Service stations are plentiful. Petrol *(gasolina)* comes in 90 (super lead-free) and 98 (lead-free super plus) grades. Diesel fuel is widely available.

Parking. Underground car parks have made parking easier in Palma (the one in Av. Antoni Maura by the Cathedral as you enter town is a good one), and it is less of a problem elsewhere. Most towns have metered areas, denoted by a 'P' and blue lines on the road.

Mechanical problems. Garages are efficient, but repairs may take time in busy areas. For emergencies, call the Real Club Automóvil (tel: 900 100 992) or tel: 062 for Guardia Civil traffic police.

Road signs. Most are standard pictographs, but you may also see the following; the subsequent phrases may also be useful.

Aparcamiento Parking
Desviación Detour
Obras Road works
Peatones Pedestrians
Peligro Danger
Salida de camiones Truck exit
Senso único One way
Useful expressions:
¿Se puede aparcar aqui? Can I park here?
Llénelo, por favor. Fill the tank please.
Ha habido un accidente. There has been an accident.

E

ELECTRICITY

The 220v system is now standard. Sockets (outlets) take round, two-pin plugs, so you will probably need an international adapter plug (available at airports).

EMBASSIES AND CONSULATES

The following are consulates:

UK: Carrer Convent dels Caputxins 4, Palma, tel: 933 666 200, www.gov. uk/government/world/spain.

US: Carrer Porto Pi 8, Palma, tel: 971 403 707, https://es.usembassy.gov.

Ireland: Carrer Sant Miquel 68, Palma, tel: 971 719 244, https://www. dfa.ie/irish-embassy/Spain.

Australia, Canada, New Zealand and South Africa have no consuls in Mallorca; their embassies in Madrid are:

Australia: Level 24, Torre Espacio, Paseo de la Castellana 259D, Madrid, tel: 913 536 600, www.spain.embassy.gov.au.

Canada: Torre Espacio, Paseo de la Castellana 259D, Madrid, tel: 913

828 400, www.canadainternational.gc.ca.
New Zealand: Calle Pinar 7, 3rd Floor, Madrid, tel: 915 230 226, https://
www.mfat.govt.nz.
South Africa: Calle Claudio Coello 91, Madrid, tel: 914 363 780, www.
dirco.gov.za.

> Where is the British/American consulate? **¿Dónde está el
> consulado británico/americano?**

EMERGENCIES
General emergency number (police, fire, ambulance)**:** 112
National Police: 091
Municipal Police: 092
Guardia Civil (traffic): 062
Ambulance: 061
Fire: 080

> Police! **Policía!**
> Help! **Socorro!**
> Fire! **Fuego!**
> Stop! **Deténgase!**
> Go away! **Váyase!**

> **G**

GETTING THERE
Air Travel (see also Airports). Palma de Mallorca's airport is linked by
regular scheduled non-stop flights from London and most other UK
cities, with frequent flights from many other European cities.

For information on scheduled flights from the UK, contact Iberia, tel: 0870 218 3848, www.iberia.com and British Airways, tel: 0844 493 0787, www.britishairways.com. From Eire, Aer Lingus, tel: 1890 800 600, www.aerlingus.com. Numerous budget airlines, including easyJet tel: 0843 104 5000 (UK), www.easyJet.com, Flybe tel: 0371 700 2000 (UK), www.flybe.com; Jet 2, tel: 0871 226 1737 (UK), www.jet2.com; Ryanair tel: 0871 246 0000 (UK), www.ryanair.com and Vueling tel: 0906 754 7541 (UK), www.vueling.com fly to Palma from airports all over the UK. Excellent bargains may be available if you travel at very short notice, both for flight-only tickets and for packages that include accommodation.

By Sea. Car ferries operate daily from Barcelona and Valencia to Palma. The slower, overnight trip takes about eight hours to Palma on Acciona-Trasmediterránea (Moll de Paraires, Estació Marítima 2, Palma, tel: 902 454 645; www.trasmediterranea.es). Baleària has services from Barcelona to Palma (7.5 hours) and to Alcúdia, which takes 6.5 hours (Moll de Paraires 3, Estació Marítima, Palma, tel: 902 160 180, www.balearia.com). It also runs a daily service from Dénia to Palma, which takes around 5.5 hours.

GUIDES AND TOURS

Local tourist offices will have details of guided bus and walking tours in the area but here is a selection of more interesting ones:

Cooltra: Carrer Monsenyor Palmer 3, Palma, www.cooltra.com. Small group tours around Palma by scooter.

Mallorca Hiking: 699 906 009, www.mallorcahiking.com. A wide range of guided walks – strenuous hikes, gastronomy, architecture – for all levels.

Mallorca Wine Tours: tel: 653 528 659, www.mallorcawinetours.com. Tours of Mallorca's vineyards on a small tourist train.

Palma City Sightseeing: 902 101 081, www.city-ss.es/destinos/palma. Open-top bus tours of Palma.

Tramuntana Tours: tel: 971 632 423, www.tramuntanatours.com. Walking, mountain biking and sea-kayaking in small groups.

H

HEALTH AND MEDICAL CARE

Standards of hygiene are generally high; the most common problems visitors encounter will be due to an excess of sun or alcohol. Bottled water is always safest, and is available, cheaply, almost everywhere. *Agua con gas* is carbonated, *agua sin gas* is still.

First-aid personnel *(practicantes)* make daily rounds of the larger resort hotels; some hotels have a nurse on duty. Many resorts have medical centres *(centros medicos)*, privately run institutions with English-speaking staff, which must be paid on the spot, in cash or by credit card (roughly €50/£45 a consultation).

Residents of EU member states are entitled to reciprocal health arrangements on production of the European health insurance card (tel: 0300 330 1350, www.ehic.org.uk available free online in your home country), but it does not cover all eventualities. Many public hospitals in Spain are refusing to accept the EHIC card so it's essential to take out insurance to cover illness or accident when on holiday.

If the UK leaves EU without a deal, the EHIC card will not be valid after the exit date. Check www.gov.uk for updates.

Pharmacies *(farmácias)* are open during normal shopping hours, but there is at least one – the *farmácia de guardia* – open all night in Palma and in the large resorts. In small towns, it may be difficult to find an after-hours pharmacy. A list of the pharmacy on rota duty is posted in chemists' windows. Spanish pharmacists are highly trained and generally speak at least some English; they can dispense drugs over the counter that would often need a prescription elsewhere.

In Palma, the Farmácia March at Avinguda Joan Miró 186, tel: 971 402 133 is open 24 hours a day, 365 days a year.

Emergency medical assistance can be obtained by dialling 112 or 061 (Ambulance), or tel: 971 295 000 – Creu Roja (Red Cross). There is also a 24-hour medical helpline, tel: 900 100 333.

Major hospitals in Palma include: Son Espases, Carretera de Valldemossa, tel: 871 205 000; and Hospital de la Creu Roja Espanyola, Carrer Pons i Gallarça 90, tel: 971 751 445.

> Where's the nearest (all-night) chemist? **¿Dónde está la farmácia (de guardia) más cercana?**
> I need a doctor/dentist. **Necesito un médico/dentista.**
> sunburn/sunstroke **quemadura del sol/una insolación**
> an upset stomach **molestías de estómago**

L

LANGUAGE

While Castilian Spanish is the national language of Spain, a local form of Catalan – Mallorquí – is widely spoken, and almost all islanders speak both. Most street signs appear only in Catalan. If you know some Spanish, you'll be fine. English and German are widely understood in resort areas.

> Do you speak English? **¿Habla usted inglés?**
> I don't speak Spanish. **No hablo español.**

LGBTQ TRAVELLERS

The Balearics are among the most hospitable places in Spain for LGBTQ travellers. Mallorca has a number of establishments, including hotels, bars, discos and restaurants that cater for the LGBTQ community or are LGBTQ-friendly. For information on the best places to go, contact Ben Amics, Carrer General Riera 3, Palma, tel: 608 366 869, www.benamics.com.

M

MAPS

The maps of the island and cities available at all tourist information offices should be sufficient, even for those travelling by car. Even though some roads are not labelled by number or name on the map, they are easy to identify.

> Do you have a map of the city/island? **¿Tiene un plano de la ciudad/isla?**

MEDIA

In the main tourist areas most English and German newspapers are sold on the day of publication. The Paris-based *International Herald Tribune* and the European edition of the *Wall Street Journal* are available on the day of publication. *USA Today* is widely available, as are popular European and American magazines.

The *Majorca Daily Bulletin* (www.majorcadailybulletin.com), an English-language publication geared mainly to a British ex-pat readership, has a What's On section. *See Mallorca* (www.seemallorca.com) is a good online resource to find out about events. For Spanish speakers, the *Diario de Mallorca* (www.diariodemallorca.es) is useful.

Most hotels and bars have television, usually tuned to sports, and broadcasting in Castilian, Catalan (from Barcelona) and Mallorquí. Satellite dishes are sprouting and most tourist hotels offer multiple channels (German, French, Sky, BBC, CNN, etc). Reception of the BBC World Service radio is usually good. English Radio One Mallorca broadcasts in English 24 hours a day on 93.8fm and 102fm.

MONEY

Currency. Since 2002, Spain's monetary unit has been the euro

(€), which is divided into 100 cents. Bank notes are available in denominations of 5, 10, 20, 50, 100, 200 and 500 euros, and there are coins for 1 and 2 euros and for 1, 2, 5, 10, 20 and 50 cents.

Currency exchange. You can exchange currency at banks (usually no commission charge) and *casas de cambio* (currency exchange stores) which stay open outside banking hours. Both banks and exchange offices pay slightly less for cash than for travellers' cheques. Always take your passport as proof of identity. Check the rates carefully prior to handing over your money.

ATMs. Perhaps the easiest way of obtaining cash but check how much your bank will charge you for doing so. Some credit card companies don't charge for withdrawing cash from ATMs abroad or for making other transactions.

Travellers' cheques. These are less frequently accepted than in years past. In 2019, there were only five places in Palma that cashed them. Check the American Express website (www.americanexpress.com) for locations.

Where's the nearest bank/currency exchange office?
¿Dónde está el banco más cercano/la oficina de cambio más cercana?

I want to change some dollars/pounds. **Quiero cambiar dólares/libres esterlina.**

Do you accept travellers' cheques? **¿Acepta usted cheques de viajero?**

Can I pay with this credit card? **¿Puedo pagar con esta tarjeta de crédito?**

O

OPENING HOURS

Most shops and offices are open from 9am to 1pm and again from 5pm until 8pm. Many museums and other tourist attractions maintain the same schedule, although increasingly the more popular ones are staying open all day. Large supermarkets and department stores usually stay open all day and some until 10pm. Banks generally open Mon–Fri 9am–2pm, and Sat 9am–1pm in winter only.

Restaurants serve lunch 1–3.30pm. In the evenings timing depends on the kind of customers they expect. Local people usually eat between 9.30 and 11pm. Places catering for foreigners may function from 7pm, and many serve food throughout the afternoon.

P

POLICE

Dial 092 for municipal police and 091 for national police. The general emergency number is 112. The municipal police station in Palma is located at Carrer de Son Dameto 1.

POST OFFICES

Identified by yellow and white signs with a crown, post offices are for mail; you can't phone from them (www.correos.es). The postal system is pretty reliable and efficient. Special delivery is always a good idea if you want to make really sure of a speedy delivery. Opening hours are usually Monday to Friday 9am–2pm. The grand main post office in Palma in Carrer Constitució 6 (off Passeig des Born), tel: 971 228 610, opens Mon–Fri 8.30am–8.30pm and Sat 9.30am–1pm. Stamps *(sellos)* are also sold by tobacconists *(estanco/tabacos)* and by most shops selling postcards. Post boxes are unmissable – large and yellow, with 'Correos' written down the side.

Where is the (nearest) post office? **¿Dónde está la oficina de correos (más cercana)?**
A stamp for this letter/postcard, please. **Por favor, un sello para esta carta/tarjeta.**

PUBLIC HOLIDAYS

The following are official public holidays. There are a number of other holidays, usually saints' days, dotted throughout the year.

1 January **Año Nuevo** New Year's Day
6 January **Epifanía** Epiphany
20 January **San Sebastián** St Sebastian's Day
1 May **Día del Trabajo** Labour Day
25 July **Santiago Apóstol** St James's Day
15 August **Asunción** Assumption
12 October **Día de la Hispanidad** National Day
1 November **Todos los Santos** All Saints' Day
6 December **Día de la** Constitución Constitution Day
8 December **Inmaculada Concepción** Immaculate Conception
25 December **Navidad** Christmas Day
Movable dates:
Late March/April **Jueves Santo** Maundy Thursday
Late March/April **Viernes Santo** Good Friday
Late March/April **Lunes de Pascua** Easter Monday
Mid-June **Corpus Christi** Corpus Christi

R

RELIGION

Spain is a predominantly Catholic country and it is important to show respect when entering a church, which includes wearing appropriate clothing (no bare shoulders, chests or short shorts).

T

TELEPHONES

Spain's country code is 34. The local area code is 971 and must be dialled before all phone numbers, even for local calls.

Coin and card-operated telephone booths were once plentiful, but as in most places have become a thing of the past. You can still make calls at the public telephone offices, which are called *locutorios*. A clerk will place the call for you and you pay for it afterwards. These tend to double as internet centres; there are a few of them spread out throughout the city.

To make an international call, dial 00 plus the country code plus the phone number, omitting any initial zero. Calls are cheaper after 10pm on weekdays, after 2pm on Saturday, and all day Sunday.

If you are going to make lots of calls within Spain it is worth buying a Spanish SIM card or new phone from a phone shop. Well-known networks are Movistar (www.movistar.es), Orange (www.orange.es) and Vodafone (www.vodafone.es). If you are using your usual phone and SIM, check with your network provider before you go that you have international roaming and find out if you can buy bundles of minutes to use abroad. It is cheaper to receive calls than to make them. Spanish mobile phones operate on GSM 900/1800 or 3G 2100.

European Union citizens can use their phones in other EU countries without incurring additional roaming fees: there is no extra charge for using your minutes, texts or data while you are away.

TIME DIFFERENCES

The Balearics keep the same time as mainland Spain, which is one hour ahead of GMT, so Spanish time is generally one hour ahead of London, the same as Paris and Johannesburg and six hours ahead of New York; it is eight hours behind Sydney and 10 hours behind Auckland.

TIPPING

Tipping in Spain is not customary but in some places it is welcomed to leave something small. A service charge is sometimes included on restaurant bills (*servicio incluido*). If not, it is usual to tip waiters 10 percent; you can leave a few coins, rounding up the bill, in a bar. Give porters, hotel cleaners and hairdressers about €1–2. It is not expected to tip a taxi driver but for exceptional service you can tip up to 10 percent.

TOILETS

There are many expressions for toilets in Spanish: *baños, servicios, lavabos, aseos, wc* and *bater*. The first three are the most common. Toilet doors usually have a 'C' for *Caballeros* (gentlemen), an 'S' for *Señoras* (ladies). Public toilets exist in some large towns but they are rare; most bars will allow you to use their facilities.

TOURIST INFORMATION OFFICES

Tourist Offices Abroad

Canada: 2 Bloor Street West, Suite 3402, Toronto, Ontario M4W 3E2, tel: 416-961 3131, www.spain.info/en.

UK: 1st Floor, 100 George Street W1U 8NU London, tel: 2011 0207317201; www.spain.info/en.

US: 333 N Michigan Avenue, Suite 2800 IL. 60601 Chicago, tel: 312-642 1992; 8383 Wilshire Boulevard, Suite 960, Beverly Hills, CA 90211, tel: 323-658 7195; Suite 5300, 60 East 42nd Street, New York, NY 10165–0039, tel: 212-265 8822; 2655 Le Jeune Rd (Gables International Plaza), Suite 605, Coral Gables FL 33134 Miami, tel: 305- 774 9643; www.spain.info/en.

Tourist Offices in Mallorca

The general information number in Palma is tel: 902 102 365.

Palma: Airport, tel: 971 789 556 for information on the whole island: Plaça de la Reina 2, tel: 971 173 990.

Municipal Tourist Offices (for information on Palma only): Square de les Meravelles Palma 07610, tel: 902 102 365; Plaça d'Espanya (Parc de les Estacions), tel: 902 102 365.

Sóller: Plaça d'Espanya s/n, tel: 971 638 008.

Pollença: Carrer de Guillem Cifre de Colonya 4, tel: 971 535 077.

TRANSPORT

Mallorca has a reliable and comprehensive transport system serving almost all towns and villages. You can get a bus and train timetable from the tourist information offices in Palma and Sóller, or tel: 971 177 771 or from a helpful information office in the Estació Intermodal (to the right of the entrance) or see www.tib.org.

Bus *(autobús)*. Buses are clean, efficient and easy to use and drivers are generally helpful. Destinations are marked on the front of the bus and each town has its own bus station or terminal. In Palma, services begin their journeys in the Estació Intermodal, the new combined bus and railway station across the road from Plaça d'Espanya. Long-distance buses are run by Transports de les Illes Balears (www.tib.org) and Palma services by Empresa Municipal de Transports (www.emtpalma. cat). There is a set fare for city journeys (€1.50) and you buy your ticket on the bus. There is also the hop-on hop-off tourist bus.

Train *(tren)*. Mallorca has three narrow-gauge lines. All of them depart and end at Estació Intermodal in Plaça d'Espanya. The first one connects Palma with Inca, the second one to Sa Pobla, while the third one will take you to Manacor. For more information visit the Transports de le Illes Balears website: www.tib.org

Metro. Palma has a metro system with two lines: Line 1 runs from the Estació Intermodal to the university and Line 2 to Marratxí. See www. urbanrail.net for a metro map.

Ferries. Car ferries run a few times a day between Port d'Alcúdia and Ciutadella in Menorca, and take around 2 hours (Baleària, tel: 966 428 700 www.balearia.com). Transmediterránea (tel: 902 454 645; www.trans-mediterranea.es) has a weekly sailing from Palma to Mahón. Baleària also runs daily sailings from Palma to Ibiza, which takes 2 hours.

Taxi. Taxi rates are metered and displayed in several languages on the window. In Palma: Radio Taxi: tel: 971 755 440; Taxi Palma Radio: tel: 971 401 414/971 702 424. In Sóller: tel: 971 638 484; In Pollença: tel: 971 866 213. In Cala Ratjada: tel: 971 819 090. On average you will pay €1 per kilometre (on weekends and between 10pm and 6am rates may be higher). Ask for a quote before you get in the car.

TRAVELLERS WITH DISABILITIES

Palma airport and most modern hotels have wheelchair access and facilities for travellers with disabilities. There are also wheelchair-friendly buses. For more general information, consult Disability Rights UK, Here East, 14 E Bay Ln, Hackney Wick, London E20 3BS, tel: 0330 995 0400, www. disabilityrightsuk.org. In Mallorca, contact Viajes 2000, Carrer dels Foners 7, Palma, tel: 971 774 684, which organises holidays for disabled people.

How much is it to the centre of town? **¿Cuanto es para ir al centro?**

V

VISAS AND ENTRY REQUIREMENTS (See also Embassies)

Citizens of the UK, US, Canada, Australia and New Zealand need only a valid passport to enter Spain and the Balearics for a stay of up to 90 days. Citizens of South Africa need a Schengen visa in order to enter Spain. Full information is available from your local Embassy. At the time of writing, the UK had not left the EU, so for UK citizens please visit www.gov.uk for updates.

W

WEBSITES AND INTERNET ACCESS

www.illesbalears.travel official tourist site for the Balearic Islands
www.angloinfo.com/balearics business directory, classifieds and what's on
   There are internet cafés in all the resorts. Many hotels, cafés and public buildings have free Wi-Fi.

Y

YOUTH HOSTELS

Good hostels include: La Victoria, Carretera Cap Pinar Km 4.9, Alcúdia, tel: 971 549 912, www.hihostels.com; and Central Palma, Plaça Josep Maria Cuadrado 2, Palma, tel: 971 101 215, www.centralpalma.com. Reserve in advance.

RECOMMENDED HOTELS

There is a wide range of accommodation available, from luxury hotels to small, family-run hostels, as well as huge, impersonal, but usually very efficient modern hotels in the bigger resorts, where much of the accommodation is block-booked by tour companies. There is also a growing number of small, stylish hotels in inland towns, many of which are delightful. Some hotels close for a few months in winter, so finding inexpensive off-season accommodation isn't always easy. For details on rural *(agroturisme)* holidays and staying in hermitages and sanctuaries, see page 114.

In 2016 a Sustainable Tourism Tax was introduced, commonly known as the "tourist tax". In 2019 it was increased, so now in addition to IVA (VAT) each visitor over the age of 16 will pay €4, €3, €2 or €1 per night, depending on the type of accommodation; there's a 50% reduction for stays over eight nights.

Some rates include breakfast and tax, but it is not standard, so it is wise to check. The following guide indicates prices for a standard double room in high season (prices should be used as an approximate guide only):

€€€€	over 250 euros
€€€	125–250 euros
€€	75–125 euros
€	below 75 euros

PALMA

Almudaina €€€ *Avinguda Jaume III 9, tel: 971 727 340,* www.hotelalmudaina. com. Established in 1972, comfortable and moderately priced, with obliging staff, the Almudaina is on Palma's foremost shopping street. Rooms on upper floors and the rooftop sky area have magnificent views over the city and the sea.

Born €€€ *Carrer Sant Jaume 3, tel: 971 712 942,* www.hotelborn.com. In a restored 16th-century palace just off Plaça Rei Joan Carles II, this hotel is one of Palma's best bargains. With a grand central staircase and beautiful courtyard under Romanesque-style arches, it is full of atmosphere. Though not in the luxury league, the rooms are charming and very comfortable. Substantial breakfast, served in the courtyard. Advance reservations are essential.

Ca Sa Padrina €€ *Carrer Tereses 2, tel: 971 425 300*, www.casapadrina. com. An attractive hotel and small (only six rooms) furnished in keeping with the converted 19th-century building in which it is set. No breakfast, but there are plenty of nearby cafés.

Convent de la Missió €€€ *Carrer de la Missió 7A, tel: 971 227 347*, www.conventdelamissio.com. This stylish hotel, in a converted 17th-century convent in the old quarter, has light, airy rooms, a roof terrace, solarium and steam rooms and an excellent, Michelin starred, restaurant, Marc Fosh.

Dalt Murada €€ *Carrer Almudaina 6A, tel: 971 425 300*, www.daltmurada. com. In a restored manor house close to the cathedral (the name means 'high walls'), this attractive little hotel has a friendly atmosphere, a garden and wood-panelled entrance hall. Advance reservations recommended.

Palacio Ca Sa Galesa €€€€ *Carrer Miramar 8, tel: 971 715 400*, www. palaciocasagalesa.com. Housed in a grand, meticulously restored 17th-century palace, this tiny hotel (only 12 rooms) is furnished with antiques, has a courtyard with fountain, and an indoor pool. Wheelchair access.

Palau Sa Font €€€ *Calle Apuntadores 38, tel: 971 712 277*, www. palausafont.com. A delightful hotel in a 16th-century episcopal palace; 19 individually decorated rooms – those at the back are quieter, but this is the quiet end of the busy street.

San Lorenzo €€€ *Carrer San Lorenzo 14, tel: 971 728 200*, www.hotel-sanlorenzo.com. This enchanting little hotel (only nine rooms) is always booked well in advance. Excellent value, rooms individually decorated; all have balconies, some have garden access. Small pool.

Hotel Tres €€€€ *Carrer Apuntadores 3, tel: 971 717 333*, www.hoteltres. com. An elegant hotel with a lovely old courtyard, a sleek bar, ultra-smart bathrooms and a rooftop terrace with a splash pool. Pets are welcomed.

THE WESTERN CORNER
Banyalbufar

Sa Baronia € *c/Baronia 16, tel: 971 618 146,* www.hbaronia.com. This endearingly simple hotel, set among terraced hills, was part of a 17th-century baronial tower. The rooms are a little spartan, but adequate; all have terraces.

Mar i Vent €€ *Carrer Major 49, tel: 971 618 000,* www.hotelmarivent.com. Attractive family-owned hotel atop a cliff with restaurant, terrace, garden, tennis court and pool. It has comfortable rooms and stunning sea views. A path leads down to two quiet coves.

Estellencs

Finca S'Olivar €€–€€€ *Carretera C-710 Km 93.5, tel: 9142 804 857/629 266 035,* www.fincaolivar.org. Gorgeous *agroturisme* set in a 6-hectare (15-acre) private valley with wonderful views over the coast. The self-catering accommodation is in two traditional stone houses and two cottages. Idyllic infinity pool with terrace.

Illetes

Bon Sol €€€–€€€€ *Paseo de Illetas 30, tel: 971 402 111,* www.hotelbonsol.es. A family-run, antique-filled hotel on multiple levels, cascading down pine-shaded cliffs to its own beach. Restaurant, sun terraces, gym, spa included.

Portals Nous

Bendinat €€€€ *Carrer Andres Ferret Sobral 1, tel: 971 675 725,* www.hotelbendinat.es. A mid-sized and handsome hacienda-style hotel in a small, rocky cove located in an exclusive area. Some of the rooms have their own balconies and there are also bungalows available amid terraced gardens. This is a great spot to base yourself in, and it is close to seven golf courses.

Port d'Andratx

Brismar €–€€ *Almirante Riera Alemany 6, tel: 971 671 600*, www.hotelbrismar.com. This comfortable and simple seafront hotel is a bargain given the coveted location. Ask for a room with a view of the harbour, although these are the noisiest. Wheelchair access. In summer three nights minimum stay.

S'Arracó

L'Escaleta €€ *Carrer del Porvenir 10, tel: 971 671 011*, www.hotelescaleta.com. Beautifully converted old schoolhouse a short distance inland from Sant Elm. Rooms are individually furnished in traditional style; there is a pool and a lovely garden where dinner is served on some evenings. Ideal for hikers and cyclists.

THE WEST COAST

Deià

S'Hotel d'es Puig €€€ *Carrer d'es Puig 4, Deià, tel: 971 639 409*, www.hoteldespuig.com. Tucked away on the stone streets of Deià this delightful little hotel has airy rooms, a serve-yourself bar and a relaxed, friendly atmosphere. Also has four apartments to let in a nearby house, and tenants can use hotel pool.

Miramar €€ *Calle Ca'n Oliver s/n, Deià, tel: 971 639 084*, www.pensionmiramardeia.com. Set above the main road up a narrow track, this pleasant little *hostal* has a cavernous entrance hall and rooms with and without bathrooms. Breakfast, which is included in the price, is served on the terrace.

Es Molí €€€€ *Carretera Valldemossa–Deià s/n, Deià, tel: 971 639 000*, www.esmoli.com. Elegant hotel in a 19th-century manor just outside Deià, with incomparable views of the village and the sea. The pool is spring-fed, and the hotel is set in 1.5 hectares (4 acres) of gardens. The service is splendid. Breakfast on the terrace.

La Residencia €€€€ *Son Canals s/n, Deià, tel: 971 636 046*, www.belmond.com/la-residencia-mallorca. Elegant hotel, owned by Belmond

Hotels, superbly located in two 16th-century manor houses. A chic international clientele enjoys a health centre, beautiful pools, tennis courts, and El Olivo, one of the island's finest restaurants.

Hostal Villa Verde €€ *Carrer Ramón Llull 19, Deià, tel: 971 639 037*, www.hostalvillaverde.es. A simple, friendly little place with a family atmosphere, situated close to the church, with a delightful garden/terrace.

Port de Sóller

Jumeirah Port Sóller Hotel & Spa €€€€ *Carrer Belgica s/n, tel: 971 637 888*. www.jumeirah.com. Opened in 2012, this five-star hotel has been described as one of the finest in the Mediterranean. With stunning cliff-top views, three gourmet restaurants, two bars, three swimming pools and a spa, who are we to argue?

Es Port €€€ *Antonio Montis s/n, Port de Sóller, tel: 971 631 650*, www.hotelesport.com. The most attractive hotel in the port, with lovely gardens, sun terraces and great views. Set a few hundred metres back from the beach, this 17th-century manor house has beamed ceilings and beautifully furnished rooms. Two good restaurants. Heated pools, thalassotherapy service.

Sóller

S'Ardeviu €€–€€€ *Carrer Vives 14, tel: 971 638 326*, www.hotelsardeviu.com. A comfortable and attractive hotel with just seven rooms and a pretty garden. It's a peaceful spot in a narrow street, although it's close to the vibrant Plaça Major.

Ca n'Aí Hotel Rural €€€-€€€€ *Camí Son Sales 50 (Cta Sóller–Deià), Sóller, tel: 971 632 494*, www.canai.com. Family-run for generations, this restored stone manor house is set in orange and lemon groves, with canals running through the grounds and the pool surrounded by palm trees; 30 suites with terraces.

El Guía €€ *Carrer Castanyer 2 Sóller, tel: 971 630 227*, www.hotelelguia.com. Opened in 1880, this pleasant, down-to-earth hotel offers excellent value. It was fully renovated in 2017 and is close to the railway station. Attractive courtyard and a good restaurant that serves typical Mallorcan dishes.

Valldemossa

Hotel Valldemossa €€€€ *Carretera Vieja de Valldemossa s/n, tel: 971 612 626,* www.valldemossahotel.com. On the outskirts of town, surrounded by orange and olive groves, this luxurious hotel is set in two 19th-century stone houses, whose rooms are furnished with antiques and artworks.

THE NORTH

Alcúdia

Ca'n Simó €€ *Carrer Sant Jaume 1, tel: 971 515 260,* www.cansimo.com. Bare stone walls, exposed beams and an attractive courtyard give this small hotel, in a converted 19th-century manor house, its character, while smart bathrooms, attractively furnished rooms and an excellent restaurant cater for all creature comforts.

Sant Jaume €€ *Carrer Sant Jaume 6, tel: 971 549 419,* www.hotelsant-jaume.com. Located close to the city walls, this hotel occupies a 19th-century 'Casa Señorial', furnished in keeping with the period. Rooms (there are only six) are individually decorated. It has a pretty patio with a fountain, and an open fireplace to cheer up winter evenings.

Cala Sant Vicenç

Cala Sant Vicenç €€€ *Carrer Maressers 2, tel: 971 530 250,* www.hotelcala-la.com. Beautifully renovated adults-only property in this stunning little bay. Relaxed but extremely efficient. The Lavanda restaurant is recommended. Wheelchair access.

Hoposa Niu €€ *Carrer Cala Barques 5, tel: 971 530 512,* www.hoposa.es. This pleasant, owner-managed hotel overlooks the lovely cove of Cala Sant Vicenç. Facilities include terraces, bar and an excellent restaurant specialising in fish and lobster. The rooftop swimming pool looks out over the sea. Reserve well in advance.

Formentor

Barceló Formentor €€€€ *Platja de Formentor 3, tel: 971 899 100*, www.barcelo.com. This classic hotel was inaugurated in 1929 and guests have included film stars, world leaders and business magnates. The garden terraces are spectacular, as are the beach and views. Three swimming pools, five restaurants, piano bar and a beauty centre.

Pollença

L'Hostal €€ *Carrer Mercat 18, tel: 971 535 002*, www.pollensahotels.com. Opened in 2005 by the owners of the Juma (below), this *hotel d'interior* is housed in a traditional townhouse, but the large rooms are modern and minimalist, with pale wood and bright colours. Shares reception with the Juma.

Juma €€ *Plaça Major 9, tel: 971 535 002*, www.pollensahotels.com. This small, smart hotel (only seven rooms), in a *Moderniste* building right on Pollença's picturesque plaza, has been keeping guests happy since 1905. Rooms are comfortable and airy. Restaurant on the ground floor; breakfast is included with stay.

Son Sant Jordi €€€ *Calle Sant Jordi 29, tel: 971 530 389*, www.hotel-sonsantjordi.com. A family hotel with character located in the heart of Pollensa. This rural property offers accommodation in restored 17th century villas. Restaurant, spa and swimming pool. Open all year.

Port de Pollença

Hostal Bahia €€–€€€ *Paseo Voramar s/n, tel: 971 866 562*, www.hoposa.es. An attractive and friendly establishment in a 19th-century summer home, with an inviting terrace, right by the sea.

Miramar €€€ *Passeig Anglada Camarasa 39, tel: 971 866 400*, www.hotel-miramar.net. An attractive, long-established beachfront hotel. The terrace has magnificent views of the bay and Cap de Formentor. Rooms have balconies but not all of them face the beach, so check when you book. Closed Nov–Mar.

Sis Pins €€ *Passeig Anglada Camarasa 77, tel: 971 867 050,* www.hotelsispins.com. This pretty, green-shuttered hotel with friendly staff is right on the beach. The bad news is that many rooms, especially those with sea-view balconies, are booked by tour operators or repeat customers. Worth a try, though.

THE CENTRAL PLAIN

Inca

Virrey €€€ *Carretera Inca-Sencelles Km 2.4, Apto Correos 490, tel: 971 881 018,* www.virreyhotel.com. This majestic mansion has been turned into a chic boutique hotel with spectacular rooms. There is a good restaurant serving Mallorcan cuisine, and a pool.

Randa

Es Reco de Randa €€€ *Carrer de sa Font 21 (4km/2.5 miles from Algaida),* tel: 971 660 997, www.esrecoderanda.com. A delightful rural hotel in a manor house, just east of Palma. Exceptional restaurant. Views are excellent, too. Book well in advance as it is popular.

Sineu

Sa Bassa Rotja €€–€€€ *Finca Son Orell, Cami de Sa Pedrera s/n, Porreres, tel: 971 168 225,* www.sabassarotja.com. A 13th-century country mansion set in large grounds, with sports facilities and a restaurant using locally produced ingredients. Ideal for a relaxing short break.

Son Bernadinet €€€ *Carretera Campos–Porreres Km 5.9, tel: 971 650 694,* www.son-bernadinet.com. A lovely manor house with minimalist decor, surrounded by almond orchards, with its own vegetable gardens, and a log fire to warm you in winter. It feels miles from anywhere, but it's only 15 minutes' drive to the nearest beach.

Celler de Ca'n Font € *Sa Plaça 18, tel: 971 520 295*. Just seven rooms, simple, comfortable and air-conditioned, in this old house, renovated in 2016. Runs a good restaurant.

THE EAST AND SOUTHEAST

Artà

Casal d'Artà €€ *Carrer Rafael Blanes 19, tel: 971 829 163*, www.casal-darta.de. A small family-run hotel in the centre of town opposite a shady square. Some Moderniste features, including good stained glass. Some rooms have four-poster beds and there's a roof terrace.

Cala d'Or

Cala d'Or €€–€€€ *Avinguda Bélgica 49, tel: 971 657 249*, www.hotelca-lador.com. This elegant hotel overlooks a semi-private cove. Friendly staff, and all the facilities you would expect. Excellent value.

Cala Figuera

Villa Sirena €€ *Carrer Virgen del Carmen 37, tel: 971 645 303/284*, www.hotelvillasirena.com. A good-value modern hotel right by the sea at the edge of this pretty village. Closed Nov–Mar.

Cala Ratjada

Cala Ratjada € *Carrer Llevamans 2, tel: 971 563 202*, www.hostalcalarat-jada.com. A pleasant little *hostal* right by the port, with en suite rooms. Book in advance.

Porto Colom

Hostal Porto Colom €€ *Carrer Cristófol Colom 5, tel: 971 825 323*, www.hostalportocolom.com. Situated right by the port, this pleasant hotel in an ochre-coloured building offers comfortable accommodation. Mediterranean restaurant and a cocktail bar with live music.

DICTIONARY

ENGLISH–SPANISH

adj adjective **adv** adverb **BE** British English **n** noun **prep** preposition **v** verb

A

abbey la abadía
accept v aceptar
access el acceso
accident el accidente
accommodation el alojamiento
account la cuenta
acupuncture la acupuntura
adapter el adaptador
address la dirección
admission la entrada
after después;
~**noon** la tarde;
~**shave** el bálsamo para después del afeitado
age la edad
agency la agencia
AIDS el sida
air el aire; ~ **conditioning** el aire acondicionado;
~ **pump** el aire;
~**line** la compañía aérea; ~**mail** el correo aéreo; ~**plane** el avión; ~**port** el aeropuerto
aisle el pasillo; ~ **seat** el asiento de pasillo
allergic alérgico; ~ **reaction** la reacción alérgica

allow v permitir
alone solo
alter v (clothing) hacer un arreglo
alternate route el otro camino
aluminum foil el papel de aluminio
amazing increíble
ambulance la ambulancia
American estadounidense
amusement park el parque de atracciones
anemic anémico
anesthesia la anestesia
animal el animal
ankle el tobillo
antibiotic el antibiótico
antiques store la tienda de -antigüedades
antiseptic cream la crema antiséptica
anything algo
apartment el apartamento
appendix (body part) el apéndice
appetizer el aperitivo
appointment la cita
arcade el salón de juegos recreativos

area code el prefijo
arm el brazo
aromatherapy la aromaterapia
around (the corner) doblando (la esquina)
arrivals (airport) las llegadas
arrive v llegar
artery la arteria
arthritis la artritis
arts las letras
Asian asiático
aspirin la aspirina
asthmatic asmático
ATM el cajero automático
attack el asalto
attend v asistir
attraction (place) el sitio de interés
attractive guapo
Australia Australia
Australian australiano
automatic automático;
~ **car** coche automático
available disponible

B

baby el bebé; ~ **bottle** el biberón;
~ **wipe** la toallita;
~**sitter** el/la canguro
back la espalda;

~**ache** el dolor de espalda; ~**pack** la mochila
bag la maleta
baggage el equipaje;
~ **claim** la recogida de equipajes; ~ **ticket** el talón de equipaje
bakery la panadería
ballet el ballet
bandage la tirita
bank el banco
bar el bar
barbecue la barbacoa
barber la peluquería de caballeros
baseball el béisbol
basket (grocery store) la cesta
basketball el baloncesto
bathroom el baño
battery (car) la batería
battery la pila
battleground el campo de batalla
be v ser, estar
beach la playa
beautiful precioso
bed la cama; ~ **and breakfast** la pensión
begin v empezar
before antes de

beginner principiante

behind detrás de

beige beis

belt el cinturón

berth la litera

best el/la mejor

better mejor

bicycle la bicicleta

big grande

bigger más grande

bike route el sendero para bicicletas

bikini el biquini; **~ wax** la depilación de las ingles

bill v **(charge)** cobrar; **~** n **(money)** el billete; **~** n **(of sale)** el recibo

bird el pájaro

birthday el cumpleaños

black negro

bladder la vejiga

bland soso

blanket la manta

bleed v sangrar

blood la sangre; **~ pressure** la tensión arterial

blouse la blusa

blue azul

board v embarcar

boarding pass la tarjeta de embarque

boat el barco

bone el hueso

book el libro; **~store** la librería

boots las botas

boring aburrido

botanical garden el jardín botánico

bother v molestar

bottle la botella; **~ opener** el abrebotellas

bowl el cuenco

box la caja

boxing match la pelea de boxeo

boy el niño; **~friend** el novio

bra el sujetador

bracelet la pulsera

brakes (car) los frenos

break v romper

break-in (burglary) el allanamiento de morada

breakdown la avería

breakfast el desayuno

breast el seno; **~feed** dar el pecho

breathe v respirar

bridge el puente

briefs (clothing) los calzoncillos

bring v traer

British británico

broken roto

brooch el broche

broom la escoba

brother el hermano

brown marrón

bug el insecto

building el edificio

burn v **(CD)** grabar

bus el autobús; **~ station** la estación de autobuses; **~ stop** la parada de autobús; **~ ticket** el billete de autobús; **~ tour** el recorrido en autobús

business los negocios; **~ card** la tarjeta de negocios; **~ cent-** er el centro de negocios; **~ class** la clase preferente; **~ hours** el horario de atención al público

butcher el carnicero

buttocks las nalgas

buy v comprar

bye adiós

C

cabaret el cabaré

cabin (house) la cabaña; **~ (ship)** el camarote

cable car el teleférico

cafe la cafetería

call v llamar; **~** n la llamada

calories las calorías

camera la cámara; **digital ~** la cámara digital; **~ case** la funda para la cámara; **~ store** la tienda de fotografía

camp v acampar; **~ stove** el hornillo; **~site** el cámping

can opener el abrelatas

Canada Canadá

Canadian canadiense

cancel v cancelar

candy el caramelo

canned goods las conservas

canyon el cañón

car el coche; **~ hire [BE]** el alquiler de coches; **~ park [BE]** el aparcamiento; **~ rental** el alquiler de coches; **~ seat** el asiento de niño

carafe la garrafa

card la tarjeta; **ATM ~** la tarjeta de cajero automático; **credit ~** la tarjeta de crédito; **debit ~** la tarjeta de débito; **phone ~** la tarjeta telefónica

carry-on (piece of hand luggage) el equipaje de mano

cart (grocery store) el carrito; **~ (luggage)** el carrito para el equipaje

carton el cartón; **~ of cigarettes** el cartón de tabaco

case (amount) la caja

cash v cobrar; **~** n el efectivo; **~ advance** sacar dinero de la tarjeta

cashier el cajero

casino el casino

castle el castillo

cathedral la catedral

cave la cueva

CD el CD

cell phone el teléfono móvil

Celsius el grado centígrado

centimeter el centímetro

certificate el certificado

chair la silla; **~ lift** la telesilla

change v **(buses)** cambiar; **~** n **(money)** el cambio

charcoal el carbón

charge v (credit card) cobrar; ~ n (cost) el precio

cheap barato

cheaper más barato

check v (on something) revisar; ~ v (luggage) facturar; ~ n (payment) el cheque; ~-in (airport) la facturación; ~-in (hotel) el registro; ~-ing account la cuenta corriente; ~-out (hotel) la salida

Cheers! ¡Salud!

chemical toilet el váter químico

chemist [BE] la farmacia

cheque [BE] el cheque

chest (body part) el pecho; ~ pain el dolor de pecho

chewing gum el chicle

child el niño; ~ seat la silla para niños

children's menu el menú para niños

children's portion la ración para niños

Chinese chino

chopsticks los palillos chinos

church la iglesia

cigar el puro

cigarette el cigarrillo

class la clase; **business** ~ la clase preferente; **economy** ~ la clase económica; **first** ~ la primera clase

classical music la música clásica

clean v limpiar; ~ adj limpio; ~-ing product el producto de limpieza; ~-ing supplies los productos de limpieza

clear v (on an ATM) borrar

cliff el acantilado

cling film [BE] el film transparente

close v (a shop) cerrar

closed cerrado

clothing la ropa; ~ store la tienda de ropa

club la discoteca

coat el abrigo

coffee shop la cafetería

coin la moneda

colander el escurridor

cold n (sickness) el catarro; ~ adj (temperature) frío

colleague el compañero de trabajo

cologne la colonia

color el color

comb el peine

come v venir

complaint la queja

computer el ordenador

concert el concierto; ~ hall la sala de conciertos

condition (medical) el estado de salud

conditioner el suavizante

condom el preservativo

conference la conferencia

confirm v confirmar

congestion la congestión

connect v (internet) conectarse

connection (internet) la conexión; ~ (flight) la conexión de vuelo

constipated estreñido

consulate el consulado

consultant el consultor

contact v ponerse en contacto con

contact lens la lentilla de contacto; ~ solution el líquido de lentillas de contacto

contagious contagioso

convention hall el salón de congresos

conveyor belt la cinta transportadora

cook v cocinar

cooking gas el gas butano

cool (temperature) frío

copper el cobre

corkscrew el sacacorchos

cost v costar

cot el catre

cotton el algodón

cough v toser; ~ n la tos

country code el código de país

cover charge la entrada

crash v (car) estrellarse

cream (ointment) la pomada

credit card la tarjeta de crédito

crew neck el cuello redondo

crib la cuna

crystal el cristal

cup la taza

currency la moneda; ~ exchange el cambio de divisas; ~ exchange office la casa de cambio

current account [BE] la cuenta corriente

customs las aduanas

cut v (hair) cortar; ~ n (injury) el corte

cute mono

cycling el ciclismo

D

damage v causar daño

damaged ha sufrido daños

dance v bailar; ~ club la discoteca

dangerous peligroso

dark oscuro

date (calendar) la fecha

day el día

deaf sordo

debit card la tarjeta de débito

deck chair la tumbona

declare v declarar

decline v (credit card) rechazar

deeply hondo

degrees (temperature) los grados

delay v retrasarse

delete v **(computer)** borrar
delicatessen la charcutería
delicious delicioso
denim tela vaquero
dentist el dentista
denture la dentadura
deodorant el desodorante
department store los grandes almacenes
departures (airport) las salidas
deposit v depositar; ~ n **(bank)** el depósito bancario; ~ v **(reserve a room)** la fianza
desert el desierto
dessert el postre
detergent el detergente
develop v **(film)** revelar
diabetic diabético
dial v marcar
diamond el diamante
diaper el pañal
diarrhea la diarrea
diesel el diesel
difficult difícil
digital digital; ~ **camera** la cámara digital; ~ **photos** las fotos digitales; ~ **prints** las fotos digitales
dining room el comedor
dinner la cena
direction la dirección
dirty sucio
disabled discapacitado; ~ **accessible**

[BE] el acceso para discapacitados
discharge (bodily fluid) la secreción
disconnect (computer) desconectar
discount el descuento
dish (kitchen) el plato; ~**washer** el lavavajillas; ~**washing liquid** el líquido lavavajillas
display v mostrar; ~ **case** la vitrina
disposable desechable; ~ **razor** la cuchilla desechable
dive v bucear
diving equipment el equipo de buceo
divorce v divorciar
dizzy mareado
doctor el médico
doll la muñeca
dollar (U.S.) el dólar
domestic nacional; ~ **flight** el vuelo nacional
door la puerta
dormitory el dormitorio
double bed la cama de matrimonio
downtown el centro
dozen la docena
drag lift el telesquí
dress (piece of clothing) el vestido; ~ **code** las normas de vestuario
drink v beber; ~ n la bebida; ~ **menu** la carta de bebidas;

~**ing water** el agua potable
drive v conducir
driver's license number el número de permiso de conducir
drop (medicine) la gota
drowsiness la somnolencia
dry cleaner la tintorería
dubbed doblada
during durante
duty (tax) el impuesto; ~**-free** libre de impuestos
DVD el DVD

E

ear la oreja; ~**ache** el dolor de oído
earlier más temprano
early temprano
earrings los pendientes
east el este
easy fácil
eat v comer
economy class la clase económica
elbow el codo
electric outlet el enchufe eléctrico
elevator el ascensor
e-mail v enviar un correo electrónico; ~ n el correo electrónico; ~ **address** la dirección de correo electrónico
emergency la emergencia; ~ **exit** la salida de urgencia

empty v vaciar
enamel (jewelry) el esmalte
end v terminar
English el inglés
engrave v grabar
enjoy v disfrutar
enter v entrar
entertainment el entretenimiento
entrance la entrada
envelope el sobre
equipment el equipo
escalators las escaleras mecánicas
e-ticket el billete electrónico
EU resident el/la residente de la UE
euro el euro
evening la noche
excess el exceso
exchange v **(money)** cambiar; ~ v **(goods)** devolver; ~ n **(place)** la casa de cambio; ~ **rate** el tipo de cambio
excursion la excursión
excuse v **(to get past)** pedir perdón; ~ v **(to get attention)** disculparse
exhausted agotado
exit v salir; ~ n la salida
expensive caro
expert (skill level) experto
exposure (film) la foto
express rápido; ~ **bus** el autobús rápido; ~ **train** el tren rápido

extension (phone) la extensión

extra adicional; ~ **large** equis ele (XL)

extract *v* (tooth) extraer

eye el ojo

eyebrow wax la depilación de cejas

F

face la cara

facial la limpieza de cutis

family la familia

fan (appliance) el ventilador; ~ **(souvenir)** el abanico

far lejos; ~**-sighted** hipermétrope

farm la granja

fast rápido; ~ **food** comida rápida

faster más rápido

fat free sin grasa

father el padre

fax *v* enviar un fax; ~ *n* el fax; ~ **number** el número de fax

fee la tasa

feed *v* alimentar

ferry el ferry

fever la fiebre

field (sports) el campo

fill *v* llenar; ~ **out** *v* **(form)** rellenar

filling (tooth) el empaste

film (camera) el carrete

fine (fee for breaking law) la multa

finger el dedo; ~**nail** la uña del dedo

fire fuego; ~ **department** los bomberos; ~ **door** la puerta de incendios

first primero; ~ **class** la primera clase

fit (clothing) quedar bien

fitting room el probador

fix *v* (repair) reparar

flashlight la linterna

flight el vuelo

floor el suelo

flower la flor

folk music la música folk

food la comida

foot el pie

football [BE] el fútbol

for para/por

forecast el pronóstico

forest el bosque

fork el tenedor

form el formulario

formula (baby) la fórmula infantil

fort el fuerte

fountain la fuente

free gratuito

freezer el congelador

fresh fresco

friend el amigo

frying pan la sartén

full completo; ~**-service** el servicio completo; ~**-time** a tiempo completo

G

game el partido

garage (parking) el garaje; ~ **(repair)** el taller

garbage bag la bolsa de basura

gas la gasolina; ~ **station** la gasolinera

gate (airport) la puerta

gay gay; ~ **bar** bar gay; ~ **club** la discoteca gay

gel (hair) la gomina

get to *v* ir a

get off *v* **(a train/bus/subway)** bajarse

gift el regalo; ~ **shop** la tienda de regalos

girl la niña; ~**friend** la novia

give *v* dar

glass (drinking) el vaso; ~ **(material)** el vidrio

glasses las gafas

go *v* (somewhere) ir a

gold el oro

golf golf; ~ **course** el campo de golf; ~ **tournament** el torneo de golf

good *n* el producto; ~ *adj* bueno; ~ **afternoon** buenas tardes; ~ **evening** buenas noches; ~ **morning** buenos días; ~**bye** adiós

gram el gramo

grandchild el nieto

grandparent el abuelo

gray gris

green verde

grocery store el supermercado

ground la tierra; ~ **floor** la planta baja; ~**cloth** la tela impermeable

group el grupo

guide el guía; ~ **book** la guía; ~ **dog** el perro guía

gym el gimnasio

gynecologist el ginecólogo

H

hair el pelo; ~ **dryer** el secador de pelo; ~ **salon** la peluquería; ~**brush** el cepillo de pelo; ~**cut** el corte de pelo; ~**spray** la laca; ~**style** el peinado; ~**stylist** el estilista

half medio; ~ **hour** la media hora; ~**kilo** el medio kilo

hammer el martillo

hand la mano; ~ **luggage [BE]** el equipaje de mano; ~**bag [BE]** el bolso

handicapped discapacitado; ~**-accessible** el acceso para discapacitados

hangover la resaca

happy feliz

hat el sombrero

have *v* tener

head (body part) la cabeza; **~ache** el dolor de cabeza; **~phones** los cascos

health la salud; **~ food store** la tienda de alimentos naturales

heart el corazón; **~ condition** padecer del corazón

heat v calentar; **~** n el calor

heater (heating BE) la calefacción

hello hola

helmet el casco

help v ayudar; **~** n la ayuda

here aquí

hi hola

high alto; **~chair** la trona; **~way** la autopista

hiking boots las botas de montaña

hill la colina

hire v [BE] alquilar; **~ car** [BE] el coche de alquiler

hitchhike v hacer autostop

hockey el hockey

holiday [BE] las vacaciones

horse track el hipódromo

hospital el hospital

hostel el albergue

hot (temperature) caliente; **~ (spicy)** picante; **~ spring** el agua termale; **~ water** el

agua caliente

hotel el hotel

hour la hora

house la casa; **~hold goods** los artículos para el hogar; **~keeping services** el servicio de limpieza de habitaciones

how (question) cómo; **~ much (question)** cuánto cuesta

hug v abrazar

hungry hambriento

hurt v **(have pain)** tener dolor

husband el marido

I

ibuprofen el ibuprofeno

ice el hielo; **~ hockey** el hockey sobre hielo

icy adj helado

identification el documento de identidad

ill v **(to feel)** encontrarse mal

in dentro

include v incluir

indoor pool la piscina cubierta

inexpensive barato

infected infectado

information (phone) el número de teléfono de información; **~ desk** el mostrador de información

insect el insecto; **~ bite** la picadura de

insecto; **~ repellent** el repelente de insectos

insert v introducir

insomnia el insomnio

instant message el mensaje instantáneo

insulin la insulina

insurance el seguro; **~ card** la tarjeta de seguro; **~ company** la compañía de seguros

interesting interesante

intermediate el nivel intermedio

international (airport area) internacional; **~ flight** el vuelo internacional; **~ student card** la tarjeta internacional de estudiante

internet la internet; **~ cafe** el cibercafé; **~ service** el servicio de internet; **wireless ~** el acceso inalámbrico

interpreter el/la intérprete

intersection el cruce

intestine el intestino

introduce v presentar

invoice [BE] la factura

Ireland Irlanda

Irish irlandés

iron v planchar; **~** n **(clothes)** la plancha

Italian italiano

J

jacket la chaqueta

jar el bote

jaw la mandíbula

jazz el jazz; **~ club** el club de jazz

jeans los vaqueros

jet ski la moto acuática

jeweler la joyería

jewelry las joyas

join v acompañar a

joint (body part) la articulación

K

key la llave; **~ card** la llave electrónica; **~ ring** el llavero

kiddie pool la piscina infantil

kidney (body part) el riñón

kilo el kilo; **~gram** el kilogramo; **~meter** el kilómetro

kiss v besar

kitchen la cocina; **~ foil** [BE] el papel de aluminio

knee la rodilla

knife el cuchillo

L

lace el encaje

lactose intolerant alérgico a la lactosa

lake el lago

large grande; **~er** más grande

last último

late (time) tarde; **~er** más tarde

launderette [BE] la lavandería

laundromat la lavandería

laundry la colada; ~
facility la lavandería; ~ **service** el
servicio de lavandería
lawyer el abogado
leather el cuero
to leave v salir
left (direction) la
izquierda
leg la pierna
lens la lente
less menos
lesson la lección
letter la carta
library la biblioteca
life la vida; ~
jacket el
chaleco salvavidas;
~**guard** el socorrista
lift n [BE] el ascensor;
~ v **(to give a
ride)** llevar en
coche; ~ **pass**
el pase de acceso a
los remontes
light n **(overhead)** la
luz; ~ v **(cigarette)** dar fuego;
~**bulb** la bombilla
lighter el mechero
like v gustar; **I like**
me gusta
line (train) la línea
linen el lino
lip el labio
liquor store la
tienda de bebidas
alcohólicas
liter el litro
little pequeño
live v vivir
liver (body part) el
hígado
loafers los mocasines

local de la zona
lock v cerrar; ~ n el
cerrojo
locker la taquilla
log on v **(computer)** iniciar sesión
log off v **(computer)** cerrar sesión
long largo; ~ **sleeves**
las mangas largas;
~**-sighted [BE]**
hipermétrope
look v mirar
lose v **(something)** perder
lost perdido; ~ **and
found** la oficina de
objetos perdidos
lotion la crema
hidratante
louder más alto
love v querer; ~ n
el amor
low bajo; ~**er** más
bajo
luggage el equipaje;
~ **cart** el carrito de
equipaje; ~ **locker**
la consigna automática; ~ **ticket** el talón
de equipaje; **hand
~ [BE]** el equipaje
de mano
lunch la comida
lung el pulmón

M

magazine la revista
magnificent magnífico
mail v enviar por
correo; ~ n el correo;
~**box** el buzón
de correo
main principal; ~

attractions
los principales
sitios de interés;
~ **course** el plato
principal
**make up a
prescription** v
[BE] despachar
medicamentos
mall el centro
comercial
man el hombre
manager el gerente
manicure la manicura
manual car el coche
con transmisión
manual
map el mapa
market el mercado
married casado
marry v casarse
**mass (church
service)** la misa
massage el masaje
match la cerilla
meal la comida
measure v **(someone)** medir
measuring cup la taza
medidora
measuring spoon la
cuchara medidora
mechanic el mecánico
medicine el medicamento
medium (size) mediano
meet v **(someone)** conocer
meeting la reunión;
~ **room** la sala de
reuniones
membership card la
tarjeta de socio

memorial (place) el
monumento
conmemorativo
memory card la
tarjeta de memoria
mend v zurcir
**menstrual
cramps** los dolores
menstruales
menu la carta
message el mensaje
meter (parking) el
parquímetro
microwave el
microondas
midday [BE] el
mediodía
midnight la medianoche
mileage el kilometraje
mini-bar el minibar
minute el minuto
missing desaparecido
mistake el error
mobile móvil; ~
home la caravana;
~ **phone [BE]**
el teléfono móvil
mobility la movilidad
money el dinero
month el mes
mop la fregona
moped el ciclomotor
more más
morning la mañana
mosque la mezquita
mother la madre
motion sickness el
mareo
motor el motor; ~
boat la lancha
motora; ~**cycle** la
motocicleta; ~**way
[BE]** la autopista

mountain la montaña;
~ **bike** la bicicleta
de montaña
mousse (hair) la
espuma para el pelo
mouth *n* la boca
movie la película; ~
theater el cine
mug *v* asaltar
muscle (body part) el
músculo
museum el museo
music la música; ~
store la tienda de
música

N

nail la uña; ~ **file** la
lima de uñas; ~
salon el salon de
manicura
name el nombre
napkin la servilleta
nappy [BE] el pañale
nationality la
nacionalidad
nature preserve la
reserva natural
(be) nauseous *v* tener
náuseas
near cerca;
~**sighted** miope;
~**by** cerca de aquí
neck el cuello
necklace el collar
need *v* necesitar
newspaper el
periódico
newsstand el quiosco
next próximo
nice *adj* amable
night la noche; ~**club**
la discoteca
no no

non sin; ~**alco-
holic** sin alcohol;
~**smoking** para no
fumadores
noon el mediodía
north el norte
nose la nariz
note [BE] el billete
nothing nada
notify *v* avisar
**novice (skill
level)** principiante
now ahora
number el número
nurse el enfermero/la
enfermera

O

office la oficina; ~
hours (doctor's) las
horas de consulta;
~ **hours (other of-
fices)** el horario de
oficina
off-licence [BE] la
tienda de bebidas
alcohólicas
oil el aceite
OK de acuerdo
old *adj* viejo
on the corner en la
esquina
once una vez
one uno; ~**way
ticket** el billete
de ida; ~**way
street** la calle de
sentido único
only solamente
open *v* abrir; ~ *adj*
abierto
opera la ópera; ~
house el teatro de
la ópera

opposite frente a
optician el oculista
orange (color) naranja
orchestra la orquesta
order *v* pedir
outdoor pool la
piscina exterior
outside fuera
over sobre; ~
**the counter
(medication)** sin
receta; ~**look
(scenic place)** el
mirador; ~**night** por
la noche
oxygen treatment
la oxigenoterapia

P

p.m. de la tarde
pacifier el chupete
pack *v* hacer las
maletas
package el paquete
paddling pool [BE] la
piscina infantil
pad [BE] la compresa
pain el dolor
pajamas los pijamas
palace el palacio
pants los pantalones
pantyhose las medias
paper el papel; ~
towel el papel de
cocina
paracetamol [BE] el
paracetamol
park *v* aparcar;
~ *n* el parque;
~**ing garage** el
párking; ~**ing lot** el
aparcamiento
**parliament build-
ing** el palacio de las

cortes
part (for car) la pieza;
~**time** a tiempo
parcial
pass through *v* estar
de paso
passenger el pasajero
passport el pasaporte;
~ **control** el control
de pasaportes
password la
contraseña
pastry shop la
pastelería
path el camino
pay *v* pagar; ~
phone el teléfono
público
**peak (of a moun-
tain)** la cima
pearl la perla
pedestrian el peatón
pediatrician el
pediatra
pedicure la pedicura
pen el bolígrafo
penicillin la penicilina
penis el pene
per por; ~ **day** por
día; ~ **hour** por
hora; ~ **night** por
noche; ~ **week** por
semana
perfume el perfume
period (menstrual) la
regla; ~ **(of time)** la
época
permit *v* permitir
petite las tallas
pequeñas
petrol la gasolina; ~
station la gaso-
linera
pewter el peltre

pharmacy la farmacia
phone v
hacer una llamada;
~ n el teléfono; ~
call la llamada de
teléfono; ~ **card** la
tarjeta telefónica; ~
number el número
de teléfono
photo la foto;
~**copy** la fotocopia;
~**graphy** la foto-
grafía
pick up v (some-
thing) recoger
picnic area la zona
para picnic
piece el trozo
Pill (birth control) la
píldora
pillow la almohada
**personal identifica-
tion number
(PIN)** la clave
pink rosa
piste [BE] la pista; ~
map [BE] el mapa
de pistas
pizzeria la pizzería
place v (a bet) hacer
una apuesta
plane el avión
plastic wrap el film
transparente
plate el plato
platform [BE]
(train) el andén
platinum el platino
play v jugar; ~ n
(theater) la obra de
teatro; ~**ground** el
patio de recreo;
~**pen** el parque
please por favor

pleasure el placer
plunger el desa-
tascador
plus size la talla
grande
pocket el bolsillo
poison el veneno
poles (skiing) los
bastones
police la policía; ~
report el certificado
de la policía; ~ **sta-
tion** la comisaría
pond el estanque
pool la piscina
pop music la música
pop
portion la ración
post [BE] el correo;
~ **office** la oficina
de correos; ~**box**
[BE] el buzón de
correos; ~**card** la
tarjeta postal
pot la olla
pottery la cerámica
**pounds (British
sterling)** las libras
esterlinas
pregnant embarazada
prescribe v recetar
prescription la receta
press v (cloth-
ing) planchar
price el precio
print v imprimir
problem el problema
produce las frutas y
verduras; ~ **store** la
frutería y verdulería
prohibit v prohibir
pronounce v
pronunciar
public el público

pull v (door sign) tirar
purple morado
purse el bolso
push v (door
sign) empujar;
~**chair** [BE] el
cochecito de niño

Q

quality n la calidad
question la pregunta
quiet adj tranquilo

R

racetrack el circuito
de carreras
racket (sports) la
raqueta
railway station
[BE] la estación de
trenes
rain la lluvia;
~**coat** el chubas-
quero; ~**forest** el
bosque pluvial;
~**y** adv lluvioso
rap (music) el rap
rape v violar; ~ n la
violación
rash la erupción
cutánea
razor blade la hoja de
afeitar
reach v localizar
ready listo
real auténtico
receipt el recibo
receive v recibir
reception la recepción
recharge v recargar
recommend v
recomendar
recommendation la
recomendación

recycle v reciclar
red rojo
refrigerator n la
nevera
region la región
registered mail el
correo certificado
regular normal
relationship la
relación
rent v alquilar
rental car el coche de
alquiler
repair v arreglar
repeat v repetir
reservation la
reserva;
~ **desk** la taquilla
reserve v reservar
restaurant el
restaurante
restroom el servicio
retired jubilado
return v (some-
thing) devolver; ~ n
[BE] la ida y vuelta
rib (body part) la
costilla
right (direction) derecha; ~ **of way** prior-
idad de paso
ring el anillo
river n el río
road map el mapa de
carreteras
rob v atracar
robbed atracado
romantic romántico
room la habitación;
~ **key** la llave de
habitación; ~ **ser-
vice** el servicio de
habitaciones
round-trip ida y vuelta

route la ruta
rowboat la barca de remos
rubbish [BE] la basura; **~ bag [BE]** la bolsa de basura
rugby el rugby
ruins las ruinas
rush la prisa

S

sad triste
safe *n* la caja fuerte; **~** *adj* seguro
sales tax el IVA
same mismo
sandals las sandalias
sanitary napkin la compresa
saucepan el cazo
sauna la sauna
save *v* (**computer**) guardar
savings (account) la cuenta de ahorro
scanner el escáner
scarf la bufanda
schedule *v* programar; **~** *n* el horario
school el colegio
science la ciencia
scissors las tijeras
sea el mar
seat el asiento
security la seguridad
see *v* ver
self-service el autoservicio
sell *v* vender
seminar el seminario
send *v* enviar
senior citizen jubilado
separated (marriage) -separado

serious serio
service (in a restaurant) el servicio
sexually transmitted disease (STD) la enfermedad de transmisión sexual
shampoo el champú
sharp afilado
shaving cream la crema de afeitar
sheet la sábana
ship *v* enviar
shirt la camisa
shoe store la zapatería
shoes los zapatos
shop *v* comprar
shopping ir de compras; **~ area** la zona de compras; **~ centre [BE]** el centro comercial; **~ mall** el centro comercial
short corto; **~ sleeves** las mangas cortas; **~s** los pantalones cortos; **~-sighted [BE]** miope
shoulder el hombro
show *v* enseñar
shower la ducha
shrine el santuario
sick enfermo
side el lado; **~ dish** la guarnición; **~ effect** el efecto secundario; **~ order** la guarnición
sightsee *v* hacer turismo
sightseeing tour el recorrido turístico

sign *v* (**name**) firmar
silk la seda
silver la plata
single (unmarried) soltero; **~ bed** la cama; **~ prints** una copia; **~ room** una habitación individual
sink el lavabo
sister la hermana
sit *v* sentarse
size la talla
skin la piel
skirt la falda
ski *v* esquiar; **~** *n* el esquí; **~ lift** el telesquí
sleep *v* dormir; **~er car** el coche cama; **~ing bag** el saco de dormir
slice *v* cortar en rodajas
slippers las zapatillas
slower más despacio
slowly despacio
small pequeño
smaller más pequeño
smoke *v* fumar
smoking (area) la zona de fumadores
snack bar la cafetería
sneakers las zapatillas de deporte
snorkeling equipment el equipo de esnórquel
snow la nieve; **~board** la tabla de snowboard; **~shoe** la raqueta de nieve; **~y** nevado
soap el jabón

soccer el fútbol
sock el calcetín
some alguno
soother [BE] el chupete
sore throat las anginas
sorry lo siento
south el sur
souvenir el recuerdo; **~ store** la tienda de recuerdos
spa el centro de salud y belleza
Spain España
Spanish el español
spatula la espátula
speak *v* hablar
special (food) la especialidad de la casa
specialist (doctor) el especialista
specimen el ejemplar
speeding el exceso de velocidad
spell *v* deletrear
spicy picante
spine (body part) la columna vertebral
spoon la cuchara
sports los deportes; **~ massage** el masaje deportivo
sporting goods store la tienda de deportes
sprain el esguince
square cuadrado; **~ kilometer** el kilómetro cuadrado; **~ meter** el metro cuadrado
stadium el estadio

stairs las escaleras

stamp v (a ticket) picar; ~ n (postage) el sello

start v empezar

starter [BE] el aperitivo

station la estación; bus~ la estación de autobuses; gas ~ la gasolinera; muster ~ [BE] el punto de reunión; petrol ~ [BE] la gasolinera; subway ~ el metro; train ~ la estación de tren

statue la estatua

stay v quedarse

steal v robar

steep empinado

sterling silver la plata esterlina

sting el escozor

stolen robado

stomach el estómago; ~ache el dolor de estómago

stop v pararse; ~ n la parada

storey [BE] la planta

stove el horno

straight recto

strange extraño

stream el arroyo

stroller el cochecito

student el estudiante

study v estudiar

stunning impresionante

subtitle el subtítulo

subway el metro; ~ station la estación de metro

suit el traje

suitcase la maleta

sun el sol; ~block el protector solar total; ~burn la quemadura solar; ~glasses las gafas de sol; ~ny soleado; ~screen el protector solar; ~stroke la insolación

super (fuel) súper; ~market el supermercado

surfboard la tabla de surf

surgical spirit [BE] el alcohol etílico

swallow v tragar

sweater el jersey

sweatshirt la sudadera

sweet (taste) dulce; ~s [BE] los caramelos

swelling la hinchazón

swim v nadar; ~suit el bañador

symbol (keyboard) el símbolo

synagogue la sinagoga

T

table la mesa

tablet (medicine) el comprimido

take v llevar; ~ away [BE] para llevar

tampon el tampón

tapas bar el bar de tapas

taste v probar

taxi el taxi

team el equipo

telephone el teléfono

temporary provisional

tennis el tenis

tent la tienda de campaña; ~ peg la estaca, ~ pole el mástil

terminal (airport) la terminal

terracotta la terracotta

terrible terrible

text v (send a message) enviar un mensaje de texto; ~ n (message) el texto

thank v dar las gracias a; ~ you gracias

that eso

theater el teatro

there ahí

thief el ladrón

thigh el muslo

thirsty sediento

this esto

throat la garganta

ticket el billete; ~ office la oficina del despacho de billetes; ~ed passenger el pasajero con billete

tie (clothing) la corbata

time el tiempo; ~table [BE] el horario

tire la rueda

tired cansado

tissue el pañuelo de paper

tobacconist el estanco

today hoy

toe el dedo del pie; ~nail la uña del pie

toilet [BE] el servicio; ~ paper el papel higiénico

tomorrow mañana

tongue la lengua

tonight esta noche

too demasiado

tooth el diente; ~brush el cepillo de dientes; ~paste la pasta de dientes

total (amount) el total

tough (food) duro

tourist el turista; ~ information office la oficina de turismo

tour el recorrido turístico

tow truck la grúa

towel la toalla

tower la torre

town la ciudad; ~ hall el ayuntamiento; ~ map el mapa de ciudad; ~ square la plaza

toy el juguete; ~ store la tienda de juguetes

track (train) el andén

traditional tradicional

traffic light el semáforo

trail la pista; ~ map el mapa de la pista

trailer el remolque

train el tren; ~ station la estación de tren

transfer v cambiar

translate v traducir

trash la basura

travel v viajar; **~ agency** la agencia de viajes; **~ sickness** el mareo; **~er's check [cheque BE]** el cheque de viaje

tree el árbol

trim (hair cut) cortarse las puntas

trip el viaje

trolley [BE] el carrito

trousers [BE] los pantalones

T-shirt la camiseta

turn off v apagar

turn on v encender

TV la televisión

type v escribir a máquina

tyre [BE] la rueda

U

United Kingdom (U.K.) el Reino Unido

United States (U.S.) los Estados Unidos

ugly feo

umbrella el paraguas

unattended desatendido

unconscious inconsciente

underground [BE] el metro; **~ station [BE]** la estación de metro

underpants [BE] los calzoncillos

understand v entender

underwear la ropa interior

university la universidad

unleaded (gas) la gasolina sin plomo

upper superior

urgent urgente

use v usar

username el nombre de usuario

utensil el cubierto

V

vacancy la habitación libre

vacation las vacaciones

vaccination la vacuna

vacuum cleaner la aspiradora

vaginal infection la infección vaginal

valid válido

valley el valle

valuable valioso

VAT [BE] el IVA

vegetarian vegetariano

vehicle registration el registro del coche

viewpoint [BE] el mirador

village el pueblo

vineyard la viña

visa (passport document) el visado

visit v visitar; **~ing hours** el horario de visita

visually impaired la persona con discapacidad visual

vitamin la vitamina

V-neck el cuello de pico

vomit v vomitar

W

wait v esperar; **~** n la espera; **~ing room** la sala de espera

waiter el camarero

waitress la camarera

wake v despertarse; **~-up call** la llamada despertador

walk v caminar; **~** n la caminata; **~ing route** la ruta de senderismo

wallet la cartera

warm v **(something)** calentar; **~** adj **(temperature)** calor

washing machine la lavadora

watch el reloj

waterfall la cascada

weather el tiempo

week la semana; **~end** el fin de semana; **~ly** semanal

welcome v acoger

well bien; **~-rested** descansado

west el oeste

what (question) qué

wheelchair la silla de ruedas; **~ ramp** la rampa para silla de ruedas

when (question) cuándo

where (question) dónde

white blanco; **~ gold** el oro blanco

who (question) quién

widowed viudo

wife la mujer

window la ventana; **~ case** el escaparate

windsurfer el surfista

wine list la carta de vinos

wireless inalámbrico; **~ internet** el acceso inalámbrico a internet; **~ internet service** el servicio inalámbrico a internet; **~ phone** el teléfono móvil

with con

withdraw v retirar; **~al (bank)** retirar fondos

without sin

woman la mujer

wool la lana

work v trabajar

wrap v envolver

wrist la muñeca

write v escribir

Y

year el año

yellow amarillo

yes sí

yesterday ayer

young joven

youth hostel el albergue juvenil

Z

zoo el zoológico

SPANISH–ENGLISH

A

a tiempo completo full-time

a tiempo parcial part-time

la abadía abbey

el abanico fan (souvenir)

abierto *adj* open

el abogado lawyer

abrazar *v* hug

el abrebotellas bottle opener

el abrelatas can opener

el abrigo coat

abrir *v* open

el abuelo grandparent

aburrido boring

acampar *v* camp

el acantilado cliff

el acceso access; **~ inalámbrico a internet** wireless internet; **~ para discapacitados** handicapped- [disabled-BE] accessible

el accidente accident

el aceite oil

aceptar *v* accept

acoger *v* welcome

acompañar a *v* join

la acupuntura acupuncture

el adaptador adapter

adicional extra

adiós goodbye

las aduanas customs

el aeropuerto airport

afilado sharp

la agencia agency; **~ de viajes** travel agency

agotado exhausted

el agua water; **~ caliente** hot water; **~ potable** drinking water

las aguas termales hot spring

ahí there

ahora now

el aire air, air pump; **~ acondicionado** air conditioning

el albergue hostel; **~ juvenil** youth hostel

alérgico allergic; **~ a la lactosa** lactose intolerant

algo anything

el algodón cotton

alguno some

alimentar *v* feed

el allanamiento de morada break-in (burglary)

alquilar *v* rent [hire BE]; **el ~ de coches** car rental [hire BE]

alto high

amable nice

amarillo yellow

la ambulancia ambulance

el amigo friend

el amor *en* love

el andén track [platform BE] (train)

anémico anemic

la anestesia anesthesia

las anginas sore throat

el anillo ring

el animal animal

antes de before

el antibiótico antibiotic

el año year

apagar *v* turn off

el aparcamiento parking lot [car park BE]

aparcar *v* park

el apartamento apartment

el apéndice appendix (body part)

el aperitivo appetizer [starter BE]

aquí here

el árbol tree

la aromaterapia aromatherapy

arreglar *v* repair

el arroyo stream

la arteria artery

la articulación joint (body part)

los artículos goods; **~ para el hogar** household good

la artritis arthritis

asaltar *v* mug

el asalto attack

el ascensor elevator [lift BE]

asiático Asian

el asiento seat; **~ de niño** car seat; **~ de pasillo** aisle seat

asistir *v* attend

asmático asthmatic

la aspiradora vacuum cleaner

la aspirina aspirin

atracado robbed

atracar *v* rob

Australia Australia

australiano Australian

auténtico real

el autobús bus; **~ rápido** express bus

automático automatic

la autopista highway [motorway BE]

el autoservicio self-service

la avería breakdown

el avión airplane, plane

avisar *v* notify

ayer yesterday

la ayuda *n* help

ayudar *v* help

el ayuntamiento town hall

azul blue

B

bailar *v* dance

bajarse *v* get off (a train, bus, subway)

bajo low
el ballet ballet
el baloncesto basketball
el bálsamo para después del afeitado aftershave
el banco bank
el bañador swimsuit
el baño bathroom
el bar bar; ~ **de tapas** tapas bar; ~ **gay** gay bar
barato cheap, inexpensive
la barbacoa barbecue
la barca de remos rowboat
el barco boat
los bastones poles (skiing)
la basura trash [rubbish BE]
la batería battery (car)
el bebé baby
beber v drink
la bebida n drink
beis beige
el béisbol baseball
besar v kiss
el biberón baby bottle
la biblioteca library
la bicicleta bicycle; ~ **de montaña** mountain bike
el billete n bill (money); ~ ticket; ~ **de autobús** bus ticket; ~ **de ida** one-way (ticket); ~ **de ida y vuelta** round trip (return BE); ~ **electrónico** e-ticket

el biquini bikini
blanco white
la blusa blouse
la boca mouth
el bolígrafo pen
la bolsa de basura garbage [rubbish BE] bag
el bolsillo pocket
el bolso purse [handbag BE]
los bomberos fire department
la bombilla lightbulb
borrar v clear (on an ATM); ~ v delete (computer)
el bosque forest; ~ **pluvial** rainforest
las botas boots; ~ **de montaña** hiking boots
el bote jar
la botella bottle
el brazo arm
británico British
el broche brooch
bucear to dive
bueno adj good
buenas noches good evening
buenas tardes good afternoon
buenos días good morning
la bufanda scarf
el buzón de correo mailbox [postbox BE]

C

la cabaña cabin (house)
el cabaré cabaret

la cabeza head (body part)
la cafetería cafe, coffee shop, snack bar
la caja case (amount); ~ **fuerte** n safe
el cajero cashier; ~ **automático** ATM
el calcetín sock
la calefacción heater [heating BE]
calentar v heat, warm
la calidad quality
la calle de sentido único one-way street
calor heat, warm (temperature)
las calorías calories
los calzoncillos briefs [underpants BE] (clothing)
la cama single bed; ~ **de matrimonio** double bed
la cámara camera; ~ **digital** digital camera
la camarera waitress
el camarero waiter
el camarote cabin (ship)
cambiar v change, exchange, transfer
el cambio n change (money); ~ **de divisas** currency exchange
caminar v walk
la caminata n walk
el camino path
la camisa shirt
la camiseta T-shirt
el cámping campsite

el campo field (sports); ~ **de batalla** battleground; ~ **de golf** golf course
Canadá Canada
canadiense Canadian
cancelar v cancel
el/la canguro babysitter
cansado tired
el cañón canyon
la cara face
los caramelos candy [sweets BE]
la caravana mobile home
el carbón charcoal
el carnicero butcher
caro expensive
el carrete film (camera)
el carrito cart [trolley BE] (grocery store); ~ **de equipaje** luggage cart
la carta letter
la carta n menu; ~ **de bebidas** drink menu; ~ **para niños** children's menu; ~ **de vinos** wine list
la cartera n wallet
el cartón carton; ~ **de tabaco** carton of cigarettes
la casa house; ~ **de cambio** currency exchange office
casado married
casarse v marry
la cascada waterfall
el casco helmet

los cascos headphones

el casino casino

el castillo castle

el catarro cold (sickness)

la catedral cathedral

el catre cot

causar daño *v* damage

el cazo saucepan

el CD CD

la cena dinner

el centímetro centimeter

el centro downtown area; **~ comercial** shopping mall [centre BE]; **~ de negocios** business center; **~ de salud y belleza** spa

el cepillo de pelo hair brush

la cerámica pottery

cerca near; **~ de aquí** nearby

la cerilla *n* match

cerrado closed

cerrar *v* close, lock; **~ sesión** *v* log off (computer)

el cerrojo *n* lock

el certificado certificate; **~ de la policía** police report

la cesta basket (grocery store)

el chaleco salvavidas life jacket

el champú shampoo

la chaqueta jacket

la charcutería delicatessen

el cheque *n* check [cheque BE] (payment); **~ de viaje** traveler's check [cheque BE]

el chicle chewing gum

chino Chinese

el chubasquero raincoat

el chupete pacifier [soother BE]

el cibercafé internet cafe

el ciclismo cycling

el ciclomotor moped

la ciencia science

el cigarrillo cigarette

la cima peak (of a mountain)

el cine movie theater

la cinta transportadora conveyor belt

el cinturón *n* belt

el circuito de carreras racetrack

la cita appointment

la ciudad town

la clase class; **~ económica** economy class; **~ preferente** business class

la clave personal identification number (PIN)

el club de jazz jazz club

cobrar *v* bill (charge); **~** *v* cash; **~** *v* charge (credit card)

el cobre copper

el coche *n* car; **~ de alquiler** rental [hire BE] car; **~ automático** automatic car; **~ cama** sleeper [sleeping BE] car; **~ con transmisión manual** manual car

el cochecito stroller [pushchair BE]

la cocina kitchen

cocinar *v* cook

el código de país country code

el codo elbow

la colada laundry

el colegio school

la colina hill

el collar necklace

la colonia cologne

el color color

la columna vertebral spine (body part)

el comedor dining room

comer *v* eat

la comida food, lunch, meal; **~ rápida** fast food

la comisaría police station

cómo how

el compañero de trabajo colleague

la compañía company; **~ aérea** airline; **~ de seguros** insurance company

comprar *v* buy, shop

la compresa sanitary napkin [pad BE]

el comprimido tablet (medicine)

con with; **~ plomo** leaded (gas)

el concierto concert

conducir *v* drive

conectarse *v* connect (internet)

la conexión connection (internet); **~ de vuelo** connection (flight)

la conferencia conference

confirmar *v* confirm

el congelador freezer

la congestión congestion

conocer *v* meet (someone)

la consigna automática luggage locker

el consulado Consulate

el consultor consultant

contagioso contagious

la contraseña password

el control de pasaportes passport control

el corazón heart

la corbata tie (clothing)

el correo *n* mail [post BE]; **~ aéreo** airmail; **~ certificado** registered mail; **~ electrónico** *n* e-mail

cortar *v* cut (hair); **~ en rodajas** to slice

cortarse las puntas *v* trim (hair cut)

el corte *n* cut (injury); **~ de pelo** haircut

corto short

costar *v* cost

la costilla rib (body part)

la crema cream; **~ antiséptica** antiseptic cream; **~ de afeitar** shaving cream; **~ hidratante** lotion

el cristal crystal

el cruce intersection

cuándo when (question)

cuánto cuesta how much

el cubierto utensil

la cuchara spoon; **~ medidora** measuring spoon

la cucharadita teaspoon

la cuchilla desechable disposable razor

el cuchillo knife

el cuello neck; **~ de pico** V-neck; **~ redondo** crew neck

el cuenco bowl

la cuenta account; **~ de ahorro** savings account; **~ corriente** checking [current BE] account

cuero leather

la cueva cave

el cumpleaños birthday

la cuna crib

D

dar to give; **~ el pecho** breastfeed; **~ fuego** light (cigarette); **~ las gracias a** *v* thank

de from, of; **~ acuerdo** OK; **~ la mañana** a.m.; **~ la tarde** p.m.; **~ la zona** local

declarar *v* declare

el dedo finger; **~ del pie** toe

deletrear *v* spell

delicioso delicious

la dentadura denture

el dentista dentist

dentro in

la depilacion wax; **~ de cejas** eyebrow wax; **~ de las ingles** bikini wax

deportes sports

depositar *v* deposit

el depósito bancario deposit (bank)

la derecha right (direction)

desaparecido missing

el desatascador plunger

desatendido unattended

el desayuno breakfast

descansado well-rested

desconectar *v* disconnect (computer)

el descuento discount

desechable disposable

el desierto desert

el desodorante deodorant

despachar medicamentos *v* fill [make up BE] a prescription

el despacho de billetes ticket office

despacio slowly

despertarse *v* wake

después after

el detergente detergent

detrás de behind (direction)

devolver *v* exchange, return (goods)

el día day

diabético diabetic

el diamante diamond

la diarrea diarrhea

el diente tooth

el diesel diesel

difícil difficult

digital digital

el dinero money

la dirección direction

la dirección address; **~ de correo electrónico** e-mail address

discapacitado handicapped [disabled BE]

la discoteca club (dance, night); **~ gay** gay club

disculparse *v* excuse (to get attention)

disfrutar *v* enjoy

disponible available

divorciar *v* divorce

doblada dubbed

doblando (la esquina) around (the corner)

la docena dozen

el documento de identidad identification

el dólar dollar (U.S.)

el dolor pain; **~ de cabeza** headache; **~ de espalda** backache; **~ de estómago** stomachache; **~ de oído** earache; **~ de pecho** chest pain

los dolores menstruales menstrual cramps

dónde where (question)

dormir *v* sleep

el dormitorio dormitory

la ducha shower

dulce sweet (taste)

durante during

el DVD DVD

E

la edad age

el edificio building

el efectivo cash

el efecto secundario side effect

el ejemplar specimen

embarazada pregnant

embarcar *v* board

la emergencia emergency

el empaste filling (tooth)

empezar *v* begin, start

empinado steep

empujar *v* push (door sign)

en la esquina on the corner

el encaje lace

encender *v* turn on

el enchufe eléctrico electric outlet

encontrarse mal v be ill

la enfermedad de transmisión sexual sexually transmitted disease (STD)

el enfermero/la enfermera nurse

enfermo sick

enseñar v show

entender v understand

la entrada admission/ cover charge; ~ entrance

entrar v enter

el entretenimiento entertainment

enviar v send, ship; ~ **por correo** v mail; ~ **un correo electrónico** v e-mail; ~ **un fax** v fax ; ~ **un mensaje de texto** v text (send a message)

envolver v wrap

la época period (of time)

el equipaje luggage [baggage BE]; ~ **de mano** carry-on (piece of hand luggage)

el equipo team

el equipo equipment; ~ **de buceo** diving equipment; ~ **de esnórquel** snorkeling equipment

equis ele (XL) extra large

el error mistake

la erupción cutánea rash

las escaleras stairs; ~ **mecánicas** escalators

el escáner scanner

el escaparate window case

la escoba broom

el escozor sting

escribir v write; ~ **a máquina** v type

el escurridor colander

el esguince sprain

el esmalte enamel (jewelry)

eso that

la espalda back

España Spain

el español Spanish

la espátula spatula

la especialidad de la casa special (food)

el especialista specialist (doctor)

la espera n wait

esperar v wait

la espuma para el pelo mousse (hair)

el esquí n ski

esquiar v ski

los esquís acuáticos water skis

esta noche tonight

la estaca tent peg

la estación station; ~ **de autobuses** bus station; ~ **de metro** subway [underground BE] station; ~ **de tren** train [railway BE] station

el estadio stadium

el estado de salud condition (medical)

los Estados Unidos United States (U.S.)

estadounidense American

el estanco tobacconist

el estanque pond

estar v be; ~ **de paso** v pass through

la estatua statue

el este east

el estilista hairstylist

esto this

el estómago stomach

estrellarse v crash (car)

estreñido constipated

estudiando studying

el estudiante student

estudiar v study

el euro euro

el exceso excess; ~ **de velocidad** speeding

la excursión excursion

experto expert (skill level)

la extensión extension (phone)

extraer v extract (tooth)

extraño strange

F

fácil adj easy

la factura bill [invoice BE]

la facturación check-in (airport)

facturar check (luggage)

la falda skirt

la familia family

la farmacia pharmacy [chemist BE]

el fax n fax

la fecha date (calendar)

feliz adj happy

feo adj ugly

el ferry ferry

la fianza deposit (to reserve a room)

la fiebre fever

el film transparente plastic wrap [cling film BE]

el fin de semana weekend

firmar v sign (name)

la flor flower

la fórmula infantil formula (baby)

el formulario form

la foto exposure (film); ~ **photo**; ~**copia** photocopy; ~**grafía** photography; ~ **digital** digital photo

la fregona mop

los frenos brakes (car)

frente a opposite

fresco fresh

frío adj cold (temperature)

las frutas y verduras produce

la frutería y verdulería produce store

el fuego fire

la fuente fountain

fuera outside

el fuerte fort

fumar v smoke

la funda para la cámara camera case
el fútbol soccer [football BE]

G

las gafas glasses; **~ de sol** sunglasses
el garaje garage (parking)
la garganta throat
la garrafa carafe
el gas butano cooking gas
la gasolina gas [petrol BE]; **~ sin plomo** unleaded gas
la gasolinera gas [petrol BE] station
gay gay
el gerente manager
el gimnasio gym
el ginecólogo gynecologist
la gomina gel (hair)
la gota drop (medicine)
grabar v burn (CD); **~** v engrave
gracias thank you
los grados degrees (temperature); **~ centígrado** Celsius
el gramo gram
grande large
los grandes almacenes department store
la granja farm
gratuito free
gris gray
la grúa tow truck
el grupo group
guapo attractive

guardar v save (computer)
la guarnición side dish, order
el guía guide
la guía guide book; **~ de tiendas** store directory
gustar v like; **me gusta** I like

H

ha sufrido daños damaged
la habitación room; **~ individual** single room; **~ libre** vacancy
hablar v speak
hacer v have; **~ una apuesta** v place (a bet); **~ un arreglo** v alter; **~ una llamada** v phone; **~ las maletas** v pack; **~ turismo** sightseeing
hambriento hungry
helado icy
la hermana sister
el hermano brother
el hielo ice
el hígado liver (body part)
la hinchazón swelling
hipermétrope farsighted [long-sighted BE]
el hipódromo horsetrack
el hockey hockey; **~ sobre hielo** ice hockey
la hoja de afeitar razor blade
hola hello
el hombre man
el hombro shoulder
hondo deeply
la hora hour
el horario n schedule [timetable BE]
los horarios hours; **~ de atención al público** business hours; **~ de oficina** office hours; **~ de visita** visiting hours
las horas de consulta office hours (doctor's)
el hornillo camp stove
el horno stove
el hospital hospital
el hotel hotel
hoy today
el hueso bone

I

el ibuprofeno ibuprofen
la ida y vuelta round-trip [return BE]
la iglesia church
impresionante stunning
imprimir v print
el impuesto duty (tax)
incluir v include
inconsciente unconscious
increíble amazing
la infección vaginal vaginal infection
infectado infected
el inglés English

iniciar sesión v log on (computer)
el insecto bug
la insolación sunstroke
el insomnio insomnia
la insulina insulin
interesante interesting
internacional international (airport area)
la internet internet
el/la intérprete interpreter
el intestino intestine
introducir v insert
ir a v go (somewhere)
ir de compras v go shopping
Irlanda Ireland
irlandés Irish
el IVA sales tax [VAT BE]
la izquierda left (direction)

J

el jabón soap
el jardín botánico botanical garden
el jazz jazz
el jersey sweater
joven young
las joyas jewelry
la joyería jeweler
jubilado retired
jugar v play
el juguete toy

K

el kilo kilo; **~gramo** kilogram; **~metraje** mileage

el kilómetro kilometer; **~ cuadrado** square kilometer

L

el labio lip
la laca hairspray
el ladrón thief
el lago lake
la lana wool
la lancha motora motor boat
largo long
el lavabo sink
la lavadora washing machine
la lavandería laundromat [launderette BE]
lavar v wash
el lavavajillas dishwasher
la lección lesson
lejos far
la lengua tongue
la lente lens
las lentillas de contacto contact lens
las letras arts
las libras esterlinas pounds (British sterling)
libre de impuestos duty-free
la librería bookstore
el libro book
la lima de uñas nail file
limpiar v clean
la limpieza de cutis facial
limpio adj clean
la línea line (train)
el lino linen
la linterna flashlight

el líquido liquid; **~ de lentillas de contacto** contact lens solution; **~ lavavajillas** dishwashing liquid
listo ready
la litera berth
el litro liter
la llamada n call; **~ de teléfono** phone call; **~ despertador** wake-up call
llamar v call
la llave key; **~ de habitación** room key; **~ electrónica** key card
el llavero key ring
las llegadas arrivals (airport)
llegar v arrive
llenar v fill
llevar v take; **~ en coche** lift (to give a ride)
la lluvia rain
lluvioso rainy
lo siento sorry
localizar v reach
la luz light (overhead)

M

la madre mother
magnífico magnificent
el malestar estomacal upset stomach
la maleta bag, suitcase
la mandíbula jaw
las mangas cortas short sleeves
las mangas lar-

gas long sleeves
la manicura manicure
la mano hand
la manta blanket
mañana tomorrow; **la ~** morning
el mapa map; **~ de carreteras** road map; **~ de ciudad** town map; **~ de la pista** trail [piste BE] map
el mar sea
marcar v dial
mareado dizzy
el mareo motion [travel BE] sickness
el marido husband
marrón brown
el martillo hammer
más more; **~ alto** louder; **~ bajo** lower; **~ barato** cheaper; **~ despacio** slower; **~ grande** larger; **~ pequeño** smaller; **~ rápido** faster; **~ tarde** later; **~ temprano** earlier
el masaje massage; **~ deportivo** sports massage
el mástil tent pole
el mecánico mechanic
el mechero lighter
la media hora half hour
mediano medium (size)
la medianoche midnight
el medicamento medicine

el médico doctor
medio half; **~ kilo** half-kilo; **~día** noon [midday BE]
medir v measure (someone)
mejor best
menos less
el mensaje message; **~ instantáneo** instant message
el mercado market
el mes month
la mesa table
el metro subway [underground BE]
el metro cuadrado square meter
la mezquita mosque
el microondas microwave
el minibar mini-bar
el minuto minute
el mirador overlook [viewpoint BE] (scenic place)
mirar v look
la misa mass (church service)
mismo same
los mocasines loafers
la mochila backpack
molestar v bother
la moneda coin, currency
mono cute
la montaña n mountain
el monumento conmemorativo memorial (place)
morado purple

el mostrador de información information desk
mostrar *v* display
la moto acuática jet ski
la motocicleta motorcycle
movilidad mobility
la mujer wife, woman
la multa fine (fee for breaking law)
la muñeca doll; ~ wrist
el músculo muscle
el museo museum
la música music; ~ **clásica** classical music; ~ **folk** folk music; ~ **pop** pop music
el muslo thigh

N

nacional domestic
la nacionalidad nationality
nada nothing
nadar *v* swim
las nalgas buttocks
naranja orange (color)
la nariz nose
necesitar *v* need
los negocios business
negro black
nevado snowy
la nevera refrigerator
el nieto grandchild
la niña girl
el niño boy, child
el nivel intermedio intermediate
no no
la noche evening, night
el nombre name; ~ **de usuario** username
normal regular
las normas de vestuario dress code
el norte north
la novia girlfriend
el novio boyfriend
el número number; ~ **de fax** fax number; ~ **de permiso de conducir** driver's license number; ~ **de teléfono** phone number; ~ **de teléfono de información** information (phone)

O

la obra de teatro play (theater)
el oculista optician
el oeste west
la oficina office; ~ **de correos** post office; ~ **de objetos perdidos** lost and found; ~ **de turismo** tourist information office
el ojo eye
la olla pot
la ópera opera
el ordenador computer
la oreja ear
la orina urine
el oro gold; ~ **amarillo** yellow gold; ~ **blanco** white gold
la orquesta orchestra

oscuro dark
el otro camino alternate route
la oxigenoterapia oxygen treatment

P

padecer del corazón heart condition
el padre father
pagar *v* pay
el pájaro bird
el palacio palace; ~ **de las cortes** parliament building
los palillos chinos chopsticks
la panadería bakery
los pantalones pants [trousers BE]; ~ **cortos** shorts
el pañal diaper [nappy BE]
el pañuelo de paper tissue
el papel paper; ~ **de aluminio** aluminum [kitchen BE] foil; ~ **de cocina** paper towel; ~ **higiénico** toilet paper
el paquete package
para for; ~ **llevar** to go [take away BE]; ~ **no fumadores** non-smoking
el paracetamol acetaminophen [paracetamol BE]
la parada *n* stop; ~ **de autobús** bus stop
el paraguas umbrella

pararse *v* stop
el párking parking garage
el parque playpen; ~ **park**; ~ **de atracciones** amusement park
el partido game; ~ **de fútbol** soccer [football BE]; ~ **de voleibol** volleyball game
el pasajero passenger; ~ **con billete** ticketed passenger
el pasaporte passport
el pase de acceso a los remontes lift pass
el pasillo aisle
la pasta de dientes toothpaste
la pastelería pastry shop
el patio de recreo playground
el peatón pedestrian
el pecho chest (body part)
el pediatra pediatrician
la pedicura pedicure
pedir *v* order
el peinado hairstyle
el peine comb
la película movie
peligroso dangerous
el pelo hair
el peltre pewter
la peluquería de caballeros barber
la peluquería hair salon

los pendientes earrings

el pene penis

la penicilina penicillin

la pensión bed and breakfast

pequeño small

perder v lose (something)

perdido lost

el perfume perfume

el periódico newspaper

la perla pearl

permitir v allow, permit

el perro guía guide dog

la persona con discapacidad visual visually impaired person

la picadura de insecto insect bite

picante spicy

picar v stamp (a ticket)

el pie foot

la piel skin

la pierna leg

la pieza part (for car)

los pijamas pajamas

la pila battery

la píldora Pill (birth control)

la piscina pool; ~ **cubierta** indoor pool; ~ **exterior** outdoor pool; ~ **infantil** kiddie [paddling BE] pool

la pista trail [piste BE]

la pizzería pizzeria

el placer pleasure

la plancha n iron (clothes)

planchar v iron

la planta floor [storey BE]; ~ **baja** ground floor

la plata silver; ~ **esterlina** sterling silver

el platino platinum

el plato dish (kitchen); ~ **principal** main course

la playa beach

la plaza town square

la policía police

la pomada cream (ointment)

ponerse en contacto con v contact

por v per; ~ **día** per day; ~ **favor** please; ~ **hora** per hour; ~ **la noche** overnight; ~ **noche** per night; ~ **semana** per week

el postre dessert

el precio price

precioso beautiful

el prefijo area code

la pregunta question

presentar v introduce

el preservativo condom

la primera clase first class

primero first

los principales sitios de interés main attraction

principiante beginner, novice (skill level)

la prioridad de paso right of way

la prisa rush

el probador fitting room

probar v taste

el problema problem

el producto good; ~ **de limpieza** cleaning product

programar v schedule

prohibir v prohibit

el pronóstico forecast

pronunciar v pronounce

el protector solar sunscreen

provisional temporary

próximo next

el público public

el pueblo village

el puente bridge

la puerta gate (airport); ~ door; ~ **de incendios** fire door

el pulmón lung

la pulsera bracelet

el puro cigar

Q

qué what (question)

quedar bien v fit (clothing)

quedarse v stay

la queja complaint

la quemadura solar sunburn

querer v love (someone)

quién who (question)

el quiosco newsstand

R

la ración portion; ~ **para niños** children's portion

la rampa para silla de ruedas wheelchair ramp

el rap rap (music)

rápido express, fast

la raqueta racket (sports); ~ **de nieve** snowshoe

la reacción alérgica allergic reaction

recargar v recharge

la recepción reception

la receta prescription

recetar v prescribe

rechazar v decline (credit card)

recibir v receive

el recibo receipt

reciclar recycling

recoger v pick up (something)

la recogida de equipajes baggage claim

la recomendación recommendation

recomendar v recommend

el recorrido tour; ~ **en autobús** bus tour; ~ **turístico** sightseeing tour

recto straight

el recuerdo souvenir

el regalo gift

la región region

el registro check-in (hotel); ~ **del coche** vehicle registration

la regla period (menstrual)

el Reino Unido United Kingdom (U.K.)

la relación relationship

rellenar v fill out (form)

el reloj watch; **~ de pared** wall clock

el remolque trailer

reparar v fix (repair)

el repelente de insectos insect repellent

repetir v repeat

la resaca hangover

la reserva reservation; **~ natural** nature preserve

reservar v reserve

el/la residente de la UE EU resident

respirar v breathe

el restaurante restaurant

retirar v withdraw; **~ fondos** withdrawal (bank)

retrasarse v delay

la reunión meeting

revelar v develop (film)

revisar v check (on something)

la revista magazine

el riñón kidney (body part)

el río river

robado stolen

robar v steal

el robo theft

la rodilla knee

rojo red

romántico romantic

romper v break

la ropa clothing; **~ interior** underwear

rosa pink

roto broken

el rugby rugby

la rueda tire [tyre BE]; **~ pinchada** flat tire [tyre BE]

las ruinas ruins

la ruta route; **~ de senderismo** walking route

S

la sábana sheet

el sacacorchos corkscrew

el saco de dormir sleeping bag

la sala room; **~ de conciertos** concert hall; **~ de espera** waiting room; **~ de reuniones** meeting room

la salida check-out (hotel)

la salida n exit; **~ de urgencia** emergency exit

las salidas departures (airport)

salir v exit, leave

el salón room; **~ de congresos** convention hall; **~ de juegos recreativos** arcade; **~ de manicura** nail salon

¡Salud! Cheers!

la salud health

las sandalias sandals

sangrar v bleed

la sangre blood

el santuario shrine

la sartén frying pan

la sauna sauna

el secador de pelo hair dryer

la secreción discharge (bodily fluid)

la seda silk

sediento thirsty

la seguridad security

el seguro insurance

seguro safe (protected)

el sello n stamp (postage)

el semáforo traffic light

la semana week

semanal weekly

el seminario seminar

el sendero trail; **~ para bicicletas** bike route

el seno breast

sentarse v sit

separado separated (marriage)

ser v be

serio serious

el servicio restroom [toilet BE]; **~** service (in a restaurant); **~ completo** full-service; **~ de habitaciones** room service; **~ inalámbrico a internet** wireless internet service; **~ de internet** internet service; **~ de lavandería** laundry service; **~ de limpieza de habitaciones** housekeeping service

la servilleta napkin

sí yes

el sida AIDS

la silla chair; **~ para niños** child seat; **~ de ruedas** wheelchair

el símbolo symbol (keyboard)

sin without; **~ alcohol** non-alcoholic; **~ grasa** fat free; **~ receta** over the counter (medication)

la sinagoga synagogue

el sitio de interés attraction (place)

el sobre envelope

el socorrista lifeguard

el sol sun

solamente only

soleado sunny

solo alone

soltero single (marriage)

el sombrero hat

la somnolencia drowsiness

sordo deaf

soso bland

el suavizante conditioner

el subtítulo subtitle

sucio dirty

la sudadera sweatshirt

el suelo floor

el sujetador bra

súper super (fuel)

superior upper
el supermercado grocery store, supermarket
la supervisión supervision
el sur south
el surfista windsurfer

T

la tabla board; **~ de snowboard** snowboard; **~ de surf** surfboard
la talla size; **~ grande** plus size; **~ pequeña** petite size
el taller garage (repair)
el talón de equipaje luggage [baggage BE] ticket
el tampón tampon
la taquilla locker; ~ reservation desk
tarde late (time)
la tarde afternoon
la tarjeta card; **~ de cajero automático** ATM card; **~ de crédito** credit card; **~ de débito** debit card; **~ de embarque** boarding pass; **~ internacional de estudiante** international student card; **~ de memoria** memory card; **~ de negocios** business card; **~ postal** postcard; **~ de seguro** insurance card; **~ de socio** membership card; **~ telefónica** phone card
la tasa fee
el taxi taxi
la taza cup; **~ medidora** measuring cup
el teatro theater; **~ de la ópera** opera house
la tela impermeable groundcloth [groundsheet BE]
el teleférico cable car
el teléfono telephone; **~ móvil** cell [mobile BE] phone; **~ público** pay phone
la telesilla chair lift
el telesquí ski/drag lift
la televisión TV
el templo temple (religious)
temprano early
el tenedor fork
tener v have; **~ dolor** v hurt (have pain); **~ náuseas** v be nauseous
el tenis tennis
la tensión arterial blood pressure
la terminal terminal (airport)
terminar v end
la terracotta terracotta
terrible terrible
el texto n text (message)

el tiempo time; **~** weather
la tienda store; **~ de alimentos naturales** health food store; **~ de antigüedades** antique store; **~ de bebidas alcohólicas** liquor store [off-licence BE]; **~ de campaña** tent; **~ de deportes** sporting goods store; **~ de fotografía** camera store; **~ de juguetes** toy store; **~ de música** music store; **~ de recuerdos** souvenir store; **~ de regalos** gift shop; **~ de ropa** clothing store
las tijeras scissors
la tintorería dry cleaner
el tipo de cambio exchange rate
tirar v pull (door sign)
la tirita bandage
la toalla towel
la toallita baby wipe
el tobillo ankle
el torneo de golf golf tournament
la torre tower
la tos n cough
toser v cough
el total total (amount)
trabajar v work
tradicional traditional
traducir v translate
traer v bring

tragar v swallow
el traje suit
tranquilo quiet
el tren train; **~ rápido** express train
triste sad
la trona highchair
el trozo piece
la tumbona deck chair
el turista tourist

U

último last
la universidad university
uno one
la uña nail; **~ del dedo** fingernail; **~ del pie** toenail
urgente urgent
usar v use

V

las vacaciones vacation [holiday BE]
vaciar v empty
la vacuna vaccination
la vagina vagina
la validez valid
valioso valuable
el valle valley
el valor value
el vaquero denim
los vaqueros jeans
el vaso glass (drinking)
el váter químico chemical toilet
vegetariano vegetarian
la vejiga bladder
vender v sell
el veneno poison

venir *v* come
la ventana window
el ventilador fan
(appliance)
ver *v* see
verde green
el vestido dress (piece
of clothing)
el viaje trip
el vidrio glass
(material)

viejo old
la viña vineyard
la violación *n* rape
violar *v* rape
el visado visa (pass-
port document)
visitar *v* visit
la vitamina vitamin
la vitrina display case
viudo widowed
vivir *v* live

vomitar *v* vomit
el vuelo flight; ~
internacional
international flight; ~
nacional domestic
flight

Z

la zapatería shoe
store
las zapatillas slip-

pers; ~ **de de-
porte** sneaker
los zapatos shoes
la zona area; ~ **de
compras** shopping
area; ~ **de fuma-
dores** smoking area;
~ **para picnic** picnic
area
el zoológico zoo
zurcir *v* mend

INDEX

pocket guide

MALLORCA

Sixth Edition 2019

Editor: Aimee White
Author: Pam Barrett
Head of DTP and Pre-Press: Rebeka Davies
Managing Editor: Carine Tracanelli
Picture Editor: Tom Smyth
Cartography Update: Carte
Update Production: Apa Digital
Photography Credits: Alamy 5M, 46; Bar Cristal
6L; Bigstock 65; Corbis 93; Fotolia 19; Getty
Images 1; Glyn Genin/Apa Publications 103; Greg
Gladman/Apa Publications 5TC, 5MC, 5M, 7, 11,
12, 15, 17, 18, 23, 26, 28, 29, 31, 33, 34, 35, 36, 38,
39, 41, 43, 44, 47, 48, 51, 53, 57, 58, 60, 62, 66, 71,
73, 74, 77, 79, 80, 84, 86, 89, 95, 105; iStock 4MC,
4TL, 5T, 5MC, 6R, 54, 69, 82, 87, 91, 100; Orient
Express 7R; Public domain 20; Robert Harding
99; Shutterstock 4TC, 4ML
Cover Picture: Hans Peter Huber/4Corners
Images

Distribution
UK, Ireland and Europe: Apa Publications
(UK) Ltd; sales@insightguides.com
United States and Canada: Ingram
Publisher Services; ips@ingramcontent.com
Australia and New Zealand: Woodslane;
info@woodslane.com.au
Southeast Asia: Apa Publications (SN) Pte;
singaporeoffice@insightguides.com
Worldwide: Apa Publications (UK) Ltd;
sales@insightguides.com

**Special Sales, Content Licensing
and CoPublishing**
Insight Guides can be purchased in bulk
quantities at discounted prices. We can
create special editions, personalised jackets
and corporate imprints tailored to your
needs. sales@insightguides.com;
www.insightguides.biz

All Rights Reserved
© 2019 Apa Digital (CH) AG and
Apa Publications (UK) Ltd

Printed in China by CTPS

No part of this book may be reproduced,
stored in a retrieval system or transmitted in
any form or means electronic, mechanical,
photocopying, recording or otherwise, without
prior written permission from Apa Publications.

Contact us
Every effort has been made to provide
accurate information in this publication,
but changes are inevitable. The publisher
cannot be responsible for any resulting loss,
inconvenience or injury. We would appreciate
it if readers would call our attention to any
errors or outdated information. We also
welcome your suggestions; please contact
us at: berlitz@apaguide.co.uk
www.insightguides.com/berlitz

Berlitz Trademark Reg. U.S. Patent Office
and other countries. Marca Registrada.
Used under licence from the Berlitz
Investment Corporation